CONFRONTATION

Also by Michael Dorman

KING OF THE COURTROOM

THE MAKING OF A SLUM

THE SECRET SERVICE STORY

UNDER 21:
A Young People's Guide to Legal Rights

WE SHALL OVERCOME

CONFRONTATION
POLITICS AND PROTEST

Michael Dorman

DELACORTE PRESS
NEW YORK

Copyright © 1974 by Michael Dorman

All rights reserved. No part of this book may be reproduced in any form or by any means without the prior written permission of the Publisher, excepting brief quotes used in connection with reviews written specifically for inclusion in a magazine or newspaper.

Manufactured in the United States of America
Designed by Jerry Tillett
First printing

Library of Congress Cataloging in Publication Data
Dorman, Michael
  Confrontation: politics and protest
  Bibliography: p.
    1. Radicalism—United States. I. Title.
HN90.R3D67   322.4'4'0973   72–7962

ISBN: 0-440-01628-2

For four Southern gentlemen
who helped teach this Yankee more about his craft
than he can describe. Alphabetically, they are:

    Jack Donahue,
    Gordon Hanna,
    Bill McIlwain,
    and Vance Trimble.

About the Author

AN award-winning journalist, Michael Dorman has worked as a reporter for *The New York Times*, *Newsday*, and *Newsweek*. He is the author of WE SHALL OVERCOME, THE SECRET SERVICE STORY, KING OF THE COURTROOM, THE MAKING OF A SLUM, PAYOFF, THE SECOND MAN, and UNDER 21: A Young People's Guide to Legal Rights. Mr. Dorman lives with his family on Long Island, New York.

CONTENTS

INTRODUCTION
Confrontation: A Form of Russian Roulette? 1

I The Struggle for Equal Rights 5
1 The Montgomery Bus Boycott 7
2 Sit-ins and Freedom Rides 19
3 Integrating Southern Universities 30
4 Riots and Reform 47

II Rebellion on the Campus 59
5 Berkeley's Free Speech Movement 61
6 Coast-to-Coast Upheaval 70
7 Tragedy at Kent State 81
8 The Aftermath of Violence 102

III The Peace Movement 115
9 Antiwar Confrontations in the Nation's Capital 117

IV Confronting the Political Process 125
10 Disruptions at the Republican and Democratic National Conventions 127

V The Resort to Terrorism 145
11 Bombers, Snipers, and Arsonists 147

CONCLUSIONS
What Lies Ahead? 161

SOURCES AND ACKNOWLEDGMENTS 169
INDEX 173

INTRODUCTION
Confrontation: A Form of Russian Roulette?

A NEW term—"the politics of confrontation" —has burst into the American lexicon in recent years. It is perhaps easier to provide examples of the politics of confrontation than it is to define the term.

When groups of demonstrators try to invade the Pentagon to protest American participation in the Vietnam war, that is an exercise in confrontation politics.

When young activists try to disrupt the Democratic National Convention to dramatize their opposition to the Party establishment, that is confrontation politics.

When white, middle-class homeowners picket the site of a proposed low-income housing project to keep poor black families from moving into their neighborhood, that is confrontation politics.

When militant students seize college buildings to protest what they consider to be repressive administration policies, that is confrontation politics.

And when self-styled revolutionaries bomb the United States Capitol, that is confrontation politics.

The dictionary is only a partial help in defining confrontation politics. It lists as one definition of *confrontation* "the act of facing in hostility or defiance." Certainly, many of those engaged in the politics of confrontation do face their adversaries in hostility or defiance. But confrontation politics is much broader than that. It embraces a wide range of activities that seek to change political or governmental policies—perhaps even the basic structure of government itself—by placing its adherents on a collision course with established law and authority. Its tactics go far beyond the usual democratic methods of resorting to such avenues of political change as the polling booth and the courtroom.

One student of the subject, Irving Howe, editor of a publication called *Dissent*, has described confrontation politics as "the equivalent in public life of Russian roulette in private life." Calling confrontation a dangerous game, Howe wrote in the *New York Times Magazine*:

> Some who play this new political game are authentic desperadoes. . . . Others are acting—or acting out—a fantasy-wish of revolution. For the desperadoes, confrontation politics can bring large risks: prison, violence, death. . . . Confrontation politics has not been well articulated as a theory. It is a kind of politics that grows up through improvisation, and it has been improvised as a way of getting around the sense of futility which has usually beset American radicalism. It has been choreographed as an out-of-doors explosion, a sort of real-life theater. The purpose is to prod and incite a dormant, insensitive society into recognizing its moral failures.

Some argue that confrontation politics is not really new to American history. What were events such as the Boston Tea Party, they ask, if not acts of political confrontation? True enough—there have been sporadic acts of political confrontation throughout America's past two centuries. But never before has there been such a wave of these acts as in recent years; never before have so many people been involved in them; in short, never before has the cumulative effect of acts of confrontation been so great as to create a new form of politics.

This book will examine the current era of confrontation politics, outlining its history, describing its major events, and seeking to assess its motivations, aims, techniques, and results. The book will also attempt to evaluate the place of confrontation in American society and predict the future course of this vital new form of politics.

The origins of present-day confrontation politics can be found in the activist phase of the civil-rights movement that began during the 1950s. Thus, that is where this examination will start.

I
The Struggle for Equal Rights

1

The Montgomery Bus Boycott

IF ONE date marked the beginning of the current era of confrontation politics, it was December 1, 1955. The place was Montgomery, Alabama, then one of the nation's leading bastions of racial segregation. On a downtown street, a woman stood waiting for the Cleveland Avenue bus to take her home from her job as a seamstress. Her name was Rosa Parks. She was a widow past the age of fifty. And she was black.

Mrs. Parks knew the segregation ordinance that governed passengers on buses in Montgomery and numerous other Southern cities. The ordinance decreed that white passengers occupied the front of the bus and black passengers occupied the rear. If there were not enough seats to accommodate every white, blacks were obliged to give their seats to whites—even if it meant standing all the way home.

In the past Mrs. Parks had always followed the rules. But this evening she was exhausted and her feet ached. As she stood waiting for the bus, a seat for the ride home seemed as precious to her as gold. At last the bus arrived. When she boarded, Mrs. Parks abided by the ordinance. She took a seat in the fifth row—the first row set aside for blacks.

For the first few minutes of her ride, she gazed out the window, paying little attention to the passengers boarding the bus at each stop. In time, all the seats were filled. Four white passengers were standing. The bus driver, a white man named J. F. Blake, looked at Mrs. Parks and three other blacks seated in the fifth row. "All right, all right," Blake said. "Come on, get in the back." The three other blacks gave up their seats and moved to the rear of the bus. But Mrs. Parks, after looking behind her and realizing that no more seats were available in the black section, did not move.

"Get out of that seat!" Blake ordered her.

"No," Mrs. Parks replied. "I won't."

Mrs. Parks had long smarted under the humiliation of obeying Southern segregation laws. Although she had not consciously decided in advance to violate the bus-seating rules, her act of defiance was no mere whim. She had served for years as secretary of the Montgomery branch of the National Association for the Advancement of Colored People (NAACP), and she was well aware that civil-rights advocates were trying to overturn segregation laws in the South. It was the combination of this long-standing racial awareness and immediate factors such as her aching feet and the lack of additional seats that made Mrs. Parks decide the time had come for a personal act of confrontation.

Bus driver Blake also recognized that Mrs. Parks's refusal to move represented more than a whim—that it was a challenge to the segregation rules. Blake sensed that she was determined, and that there was no use arguing with her. He felt that the only thing he could do was stop the bus and look for a policeman. A few minutes after leaving the bus, Blake returned with an officer and found Mrs. Parks still in her seat. The officer pulled her out of the seat by her arms. "What are you taking me in for?" Mrs. Parks asked. "What did I do against the law?" The policeman pushed her ahead of him, out of the bus, and placed her under arrest on a charge of violating a city law providing for racial segregation on publicly owned vehicles. Mrs. Parks was taken to police headquarters and placed in a jail cell. From the jail, she telephoned a plea for help to a black man named E. D. Nixon, who had long been a leader in struggles to obtain better treatment for Montgomery's blacks. Nixon quickly posted bond for Mrs. Parks, and she was released.

By then word of the arrest had spread swiftly through the black community. For some time Montgomery's black leaders had been considering a legal challenge to the segregated-seating policy on the buses, and had been trying to work out a strategy for their campaign. When Nixon bailed out Mrs. Parks, he told her, "This is what we've been waiting for." He felt her arrest would provide the vehicle for a clear-cut test of whether the Montgomery segregation laws violated the Fourteenth Amendment to the United States Constitution, which guarantees every American equal protection under the law. Although other blacks had previously been arrested for refusing to abide by the Montgomery segregation laws, police had avoided court tests of the statutes by charging most of the defendants with disorderly conduct, rather than with disobeying the segregation laws themselves. Nixon asked Mrs. Parks if she would cooperate in a symbolic case challenging the segregation laws, even if it meant the loss of her job and other harassment. She said she would.

In addition to fighting Mrs. Parks's case in the courts, Nixon and other black leaders decided to mount a direct-action campaign against the bus-segregation policy. They would organize a one-day boycott of the bus system by all Montgomery blacks to demonstrate to the city's white establishment the potential political and economic power of the black community. Although the one-day boycott would not cause the bus lines major financial losses, if successfully organized it would serve as a warning of possible future boycotts should the demands of the black citizens continue to be ignored. Since blacks formed the majority of Montgomery's bus-riding public, a long-term boycott could prove financially disastrous to the bus lines.

All night following Mrs. Parks's arrest, Nixon stayed on the telephone, calling everyone he thought could be helpful in planning the boycott. Among those he phoned was the new, young minister at the Dexter Avenue Baptist Church, Dr. Martin Luther King, Jr. At that time, Dr. King was scarcely well known in Montgomery, much less in other parts of the country. He had taken over the Dexter Avenue pastorate little more than a year earlier, and had devoted most of his time to his church. He had not been particularly active in desegregation work. When Nixon asked him to become a member of the committee planning the one-day bus boycott, King hesitated at first but finally agreed. The decision was a milestone in King's career, leading him toward his destiny as the best-known black spokesman in the country.

Nixon's committee chose to stage the boycott on December 5, the day Mrs. Parks was scheduled to stand trial. Thousands of leaflets urging blacks to take part in the boycott were printed and distributed in the black community. On the day before the boycott, ministers of black churches throughout Montgomery urged their parishioners to participate. Meanwhile, a member of the planning committee called on the city's eighteen black taxi companies and persuaded them to drive groups of blacks at reduced fares on the day of the boycott.

Word of the boycott was spread by the news media, but generally whites greeted it with apathy. They saw little danger in a one-day boycott, assuming that it would soon be over and forgotten. Some of the more militant segregationists denounced the plan, but they attracted little attention.

On December 5 the buses rolling through the black sections of Montgomery were empty. Students walked or hitched rides. Other people drove, rode with friends or in taxis, or walked. A few blacks even rode horses and mules.

Meanwhile, at mid-morning Mrs. Parks appeared in court for trial. The city prosecutor argued that the facts of the case clearly proved Mrs. Parks had violated the local laws requiring segregated seating on the buses. The judge found Mrs. Parks guilty and fined her ten dollars plus four dollars in court costs. Her attorney filed notice that the conviction would be appealed to a higher state court. The appeal would provide an opportunity to test the constitutionality of the segregation laws.

That afternoon members of the committee that had planned the boycott met and formed an organization known as the Montgomery Improvement Association. While the organization made no immediate demand for desegregation on the buses, it hoped to continue the boycott until three basic demands were met: courtesy toward black passengers on the part of the bus lines; seating on a first-come, first-served basis, with blacks sitting from the back toward the front of the buses and whites from the front toward the back; and hiring of black drivers on routes that served predominantly black areas.

As a head for the new organization, black leaders sought a dynamic speaker with recognized intelligence and high character, if possible someone who had not been active in Montgomery's black community long enough to have made many enemies. Dr. Martin Luther King, Jr., met all those qualifications. Dr. King was surprised when his name was placed in nomination for the presidency of the organization but he attributed little importance to it, assuming there would be other nominations and that someone else would be elected. He was mistaken. No one else's name was offered, the nominations were closed, and a flabbergasted Dr. King found himself elected unanimously. He later told friends that, had he been given time to think through the consequences, he would have declined the nomination. As the new minister of his church, he felt that his parish required most of his attention. But now, like it or not, he was on his way to becoming a civil-rights leader.

That night, hundreds of blacks jammed into a church for a mass meeting sponsored by the Montgomery Improvement Association. Another four thousand blacks stood outside on the streets. Dr. King, as president of the new organization, was chief speaker. "There comes a time when people get tired—tired of being segregated and humiliated, tired of being kicked about by the brutal feet of oppression!" he declared. "One of the great glories of democracy is the right to protest for right. The White Citizens Councils and the Ku Klux Klan are protesting for the perpetuation of injustice in the community. Their methods lead to violence and lawlessness. But in our protest there will be no cross burnings. No white person will be taken from his home by a hooded Negro mob and brutally murdered. There will be no threats and intimidation. We will be guided by the highest principles of law and order. . . . If you will protest courageously and yet with dignity and Christian love, when the history books are written in future generations the historians will have to pause and say: 'There lived a great people—a black people—who injected new meaning and dignity into the veins of civilization.' This is our challenge and our overwhelming responsibility."

A roar of approval greeted the speech. When the gathering was asked to vote on the three-point set of demands to be issued to city officials and the bus lines, every person in the church stood to signify support. As Dr. King later wrote: "The people had expressed their determination not to ride the buses until conditions were changed."

Thus, the boycott was extended beyond the one day. It was no simple matter to arrange the logistics of getting blacks to and from work, school, and other locations on a continuing basis. In the past, about 17,500 blacks had ridden the buses at least twice daily in Montgomery. Now, through a massive campaign of cooperation, they found other means. Each day the buses rolled through the black areas and returned empty. The boycott was costing the company that owned the bus lines $7,000 a day. In addition, downtown merchants complained that, as an indirect result of the boycott, sales were dropping substantially, even though it was the pre-Christmas shopping season.

Many whites reacted with outrage. Housewives were angry because they had to drive into black neighborhoods to pick up their housekeepers. Other whites were angry over the financial losses being suffered by the bus lines and merchants. Some ordered their black employees to ride the buses or be fired. Almost without exception, blacks refused to ride the buses. Some were fired, but it quickly became obvious that such tactics could not break the boycott.

Meanwhile, attempts were made to mediate the dispute. Officials of the bus lines, the city, and the Montgomery Improvement Association met several times—but the whites would not accept all the black demands, and the blacks refused to back down. Leaders of the white community responded by trying to harass the blacks into submission. City officials notified the black taxi companies that mass riding was illegal and their franchises could be taken away if they continued cooperating with the boycotting blacks. This action brought the movement new publicity, and financial contributions started pouring in from all parts of the country. With the money, the Montgomery Improvement Association bought ten station wagons and formed a car pool for boycotters. A number of city officials, including Mayor W. A. Gayle, responded by joining the segregationist White Citizens Council.

Next, Dr. King was arrested on a traffic charge by policemen who had been following him with the apparent intention of "getting something" on him. Although he had been taking special care to drive slowly, the officers charged him with going thirty miles an hour in a twenty-five-mile zone, and instead of merely giving him a ticket, they hauled him off to jail. When friends of Dr. King tried to bail him out, they were told he would have to remain in jail overnight.

The Reverend Ralph Abernathy, who was to be a longtime associate of Dr. King, feared that harm might come to his friend in jail. Abernathy decided to employ further confrontation strategy. He quickly organized a protest demonstration outside the jail. The warden, seeing scores of blacks outside his institution, and fearing an outbreak of violence, reversed the earlier decision and released Dr. King.

The confrontation at the jail escalated attempts to break the boycott. Angry whites bombed the homes of Dr. King and other boycott leaders, and several black churches. The White Citizens Council whipped up racist sentiment against the boycott. Among other activities, the Council distributed leaflets that read in part: "When in the course of human events it becomes necessary to abolish the Negro race, proper methods should be used. Among these are guns, bows and arrows, slingshots and knives."

Such harassment merely bolstered the boycotters' determination. Far from backing down, they stiffened their demands for ending the boycott. Now they insisted on total abandonment of the segregated-seating rules on the buses.

The boycott dragged on, week after week, and the positions of both sides hardened.

As a followup on the demand for desegregation of bus seating, four black women who were participating in the boycott filed a federal court suit testing the constitutionality of the segregation policy. Mrs. Rosa Parks's appeal of her conviction, while also contending the policy was unconstitutional, sought to invalidate criminal charges based on the segregation laws, but it could not have the direct effect of bringing about court-ordered desegregation of the buses. Only a civil suit could do so. The suit filed by the four other women sought such a court order.

A federal district court ruled in favor of the four women, but the decision was appealed by city officials, who were under heavy pressure to bring a halt to the boycott. White merchants complained that they had lost almost $1 million in sales during the first three months of the boycott. The company operating the bus lines claimed it had lost $225,000 and thus could not afford to pay the $20,000 it owed the city in taxes.

Against that background, the officials filed a barrage of suits against the Montgomery Improvement Association. One suit asked for a ban on further operation of the Association's car pool, claiming it was an unlicensed transit system. Another asked the state courts to bar the Association from spending any additional money.

Meanwhile, the four black women's suit seeking to ban segregation on the buses made its way through the judicial maze to the U.S. Supreme Court. While the Supreme Court was considering the case, a state-court trial opened in Montgomery on the city's suit to ban the car pool. By that time it was November 13, 1956. The boycott had been in effect almost a year.

As Dr. King sat in court, listening to opposing arguments

in the car-pool case, a newsman slipped up beside him, handed him an Associated Press news bulletin, and said, "Here is the decision you have been waiting for. Read this release." The bulletin said that the Supreme Court had just upheld the lower court's decision in the four women's case, which declared unconstitutional Alabama's state and local laws requiring segregation on buses. The decision held that the segregation requirements violated the Fourteenth Amendment. Ultimately it led to the reversal of Mrs. Parks's conviction. For all intents and purposes, the Supreme Court ruling meant that Dr. King and his supporters had won the battle that had begun with Mrs. Parks's refusal to give up her seat on the bus.

There were additional skirmishes, to be sure. Montgomery city officials won their case barring further use of the car pool, but it was a hollow victory. A delay of several weeks occurred before the Supreme Court ruling took effect, so the segregation policy and the boycott remained in operation, but city officials issued a statement making it clear that, while they did not like the ruling, they would be compelled to obey it.

By December 20 the Supreme Court decision had been served on city officials, and Dr. King told a mass meeting that the boycott was over. "The Negro citizens of Montgomery are urged to return to the buses tomorrow morning on a nonsegregated basis," he said. "We must act in such a way as to make possible a coming together of white people and colored people on the basis of a real harmony of interests and understanding. We seek an integration based on mutual respect."

At 5 o'clock the next morning, a small group met in Dr. King's home. Among those present were the Reverend Ralph Abernathy and a white minister, Dr. Glenn Smiley. At 5:55 the three men walked out to the street and waited at a bus stop. Minutes later, an empty bus pulled up. The driver, a white man, opened the door and asked with a broad smile, "I believe you are the Reverend King, aren't you?"

"Yes, I am."

"We are glad to have you this morning," the driver said.

King and Smiley took seats side by side near the front of the bus. Abernathy sat ahead of them, to be joined shortly by a black woman. Thus, the first desegregated bus in Montgomery's history rolled through the black area toward the downtown section. Outside of a few relatively mild protests from white passengers, the first day of bus integration passed without trouble. In succeeding days, weeks, and months, there were scattered outbreaks of racial violence in Montgomery, but no amount of violence could alter the truth: The desegregation of the buses was an accomplished fact.

Several distinct acts of political confrontation had taken place during the Montgomery dispute—including Mrs. Parks's original refusal to leave her seat, the organization and imposition of the bus boycott, the demonstration outside the jail to protest Dr. King's arrest, and the refusal of the black leaders to yield to official pressure and end the boycott before their demands had been satisfied. Why was the campaign successful? Partly, at least, it was because the black leaders combined their acts of confrontation with resort to the time-honored system of redressing grievances: the court system. The confrontations mobilized public support, raised money for the various court battles, and helped prepare a moral climate in which desegregation seemed inevitable.

There were other, equally important reasons for the success of the campaign. For one, Dr. King and his associates directed their acts of confrontation at very specific, attainable goals. For another, they exercised great discipline over their followers, persuading them to forsake violence in the interest of winning the long-range struggle. For still another, they demonstrated that black economic power could be converted into a formidable weapon in the politics of confrontation.

Compared with later episodes in the history of confrontation politics, the Montgomery boycott might seem lacking in drama. There were no massive confrontations in the streets between members of opposing forces. There were no large-scale sweeps by club-swinging policemen, no serious blood-lettings, no mass arrests. Yet the boycott was immensely significant. Not only did it establish Dr. King as a civil-rights leader of national importance, it touched off what has come to be known as "the black revolution," and, as previously noted, marked the beginning of the current era of confrontation politics. After Montgomery there was no turning back, for either the black revolution or the confrontation era of which it became a part.

2

Sit-ins and Freedom Rides

THE success of the Montgomery boycott inspired blacks in other cities across the South to adopt the politics of confrontation as a means of seeking rights long denied them. Their protests were not always so effective as the one in Montgomery. They suffered some setbacks. But they continued to press their demands.

It was not until February 1, 1960—more than three years after the end of the Montgomery boycott—that the event described by the late author Louis Lomax as "the second major battle of the Negro revolt" began. On that date, four students at the all-black Agricultural and Technical College in Greensboro, North Carolina, entered a local five-and-dime store and sat down at a lunch counter open exclusively to whites. They were ordered to leave, but they refused. The store manager closed the counter. Still the students would not budge. They opened their school books and began to study. For the next two and a half hours, they remained at the counter. Thus began what came to be known as "the sit-in movement."

The police were not called, and no attempts were made to remove the students by force. After the two and a half hours, they closed their books and left. But they returned on the following two days with additional students, each time repeating their performance.

In Greensboro, as in many other Southern cities, public eating facilities such as lunch counters were segregated by law. In 1954, in its decision in the case of *Brown v. Board of Education*, the Supreme Court had ruled that "separate but equal" public schools for black and white students were unconstitutional. It had followed up that decision by ruling in the Montgomery case that laws requiring segregation on public buses were also invalid. But no test case had yet reached the Court on the issue of such segregated facilities as restaurants and lunch counters.

In Greensboro, the black students were joined on the fourth day of the sit-in by white students from the Women's College of the University of North Carolina. The white students sat down at the counter, but refused to order food unless the blacks also were served. Once again, the store manager closed the counter.

Although the sit-in had developed more or less spontaneously, much as had Mrs. Parks's refusal to leave her bus seat, the students realized they would need organizational support if they were to continue the protest for more than a few days. With the help of a local black leader, they enlisted the aid of the national headquarters of a civil-rights group named the Congress of Racial Equality (CORE).

CORE, which had been in existence for twenty years, had recently begun using confrontation tactics in civil-rights demonstrations. The national headquarters sent a team of field workers to Greensboro to train black students in the philosophy and technique of nonviolent confrontation. The field workers organized training sessions at which they played the roles of white segregationists and the students, seated at a simulated lunch counter, pretended they were taking part in sit-ins. The field workers called the students vile names, blew cigarette smoke into their eyes, shoved them, and, when the students still failed to react, punched them. Any student who struck back or "lost his cool" was eliminated from the course. Only those who sat stolidly through the most severe harassment, making no attempt to retaliate, were permitted to participate in actual sit-ins.

When the Greensboro protest started drawing national publicity, other civil-rights groups sent help to the students. Among those who arrived to lend his prestige and counsel to the sit-in was Dr. Martin Luther King, Jr., who by that time had become president of a new organization known as the Southern Christian Leadership Conference. SCLC, which was organizing nonviolent protests in various parts of the South, sent aides to advise the Greensboro students. Later, the NAACP also sent an adviser. The Greensboro movement suffered a series of setbacks, but eventually succeeded in winning concessions permitting desegregated use of some facilities.

Meanwhile, college students in other cities and states launched sit-ins of their own. In Durham, North Carolina, black students from North Carolina College and whites from Duke University sat in at a segregated restaurant. A similar sit-in was staged in Winston-Salem, North Carolina, by blacks from Teachers College and whites from Wake Forest University. The movement then spread to every state in the Deep South and such other states as Ohio, Illinois and Nevada.

Ultimately, the sit-ins involved more participants than any previous civil-rights movement. More than 70,000 blacks and whites took part. There were at least 800 sit-ins in more than 100 cities. More than 4,000 demonstrators were arrested. In many cases, the demonstrators were beaten by white segregationists and/or policemen. At a peaceful demonstration involving about 750 students in Orangeburg, South Carolina, policemen bombarded the students with tear-gas grenades and firemen turned fire hoses on them, knocking them to the ground. More than 500 of the students were arrested. Similar incidents occurred in other cities.

In some cities the operators of restaurants and lunch counters agreed to desegregate. In many others, however, they refused. Some even shut down their restaurants or lunch counters, rather than see them desegregated. By and large, at the end of the decade eating facilities in the South and some border states remained segregated.

Throughout 1960 and into 1961, sit-ins continued in one city after another. Meanwhile, suits were filed to bring about court-ordered desegregation of public eating places such as restaurants and lunch counters. Another outgrowth of the sit-in movement was the formation of a new civil-rights group composed chiefly of students: the Student Nonviolent Coordinating Committee (SNCC), with headquarters in Atlanta.

In the spring of 1961, officials of CORE, SNCC, and SCLC met jointly and decided to expand the sit-in movement with a series of segregation challenges to be known as Freedom Rides. The guiding hand behind the Freedom Rides belonged to James Farmer, a former Methodist minister who had recently become national director of CORE. The rides would be designed to test laws and customs that provided for segregated lunch counters, rest rooms, waiting rooms, drinking fountains, and other facilities at bus depots in the South. Members of the three cooperating organizations, but chiefly students from SNCC, would board buses in Washington, D.C., and ride south. Along the way, white participants would try to use black facilities and black riders would try to use white facilities.

Once again, this would involve exercises in the politics of confrontation. On the surface, a white man entering a men's room marked "colored men" might not seem to be engaging in a very dramatic act. But if entering that door were a violation of local or state law, he might well be risking a beating at the hands of white civilians or policemen, or arrest and imprisonment. The Freedom Riders would be trained in nonviolent protest and would be expected to refrain from retaliating if subjected to harassment or violence. If they were arrested, their cases would provide a way to challenge various segregation laws in the courts. If they were refused service at bus-depot lunch counters, there would be additional grounds for lawsuits.

The first Freedom Riders left Washington on May 4, 1961, one group on a Greyhound bus and another on a Trailways bus. The groups, each composed of about a dozen blacks and whites, planned to travel through Virginia, North Carolina, South Carolina, Georgia, Alabama, and Mississippi. City officials were expecting them at each stop along the line, but the reception accorded them varied from place to place. In some cases the riders were allowed to desegregate facilities without obstruction. In some cities they found the lunch counters closed. In others the counters were open but service was deliberately kept so slow that the riders could not eat and still make it back to the buses in time to leave. In still others some of the riders were arrested on charges of violating segregation or disorderly-conduct laws.

What follows is a partial chronology of the Freedom Rides, reporting on some of the more important events:

Late on May 13, the two groups of Freedom Riders arrived in Atlanta. The restaurant at the Greyhound terminal had been closed to prevent it from being desegregated, but some of the riders were served in the restaurant at the Trailways terminal without incident.

The two groups then left in separate buses for Birmingham, Alabama. While they were en route, United States Justice Department officials received confidential information that white segregationists—including members of the Ku Klux Klan—planned assaults on the riders in Alabama. This information was passed on to Alabama officials, but they took no precautions to protect the riders. Near Anniston, Alabama, a mob of whites blocked a highway and stopped the Greyhound bus. The mob broke the bus windows with clubs, sending glass splattering over the passengers, and hurled a firebomb inside, forcing the driver and riders to flee; as they jumped from the bus, they were beaten by the mob. Twelve of them were hospitalized.

When the Trailways bus reached Anniston, it too was intercepted by a mob. Eight toughs carrying tire irons and clubs boarded the bus and beat the riders. They ordered the driver to take the bus directly to Birmingham, without stopping to allow the injured passengers to be treated. Although news of the attacks reached Birmingham well before the riders arrived, no police were on hand when the Trailways bus pulled into the Birmingham terminal—but there was another white mob present. The toughs aboard the bus forced the passengers to walk out into the mob, and they were beaten again, sometimes savagely. Police did not arrive until ten minutes after the attack began, and even then they did not make any arrests. Nor had the police in Anniston made any arrests.

Eventually the Justice Department ordered the FBI to investigate the Anniston attacks, and several arrests were made. The defendants were charged with violating federal laws by firebombing and otherwise damaging the buses. In addition, Justice Department lawyers obtained a federal-court injunction barring various Ku Klux Klan groups and their leaders from further interference with the Freedom Rides.

The attacks in Anniston and Birmingham did not end the

Freedom Rides, but a temporary halt to activity was called when the Greyhound and Trailways lines refused to provide the two groups of riders with further transportation. The bus lines said they could not afford additional losses of equipment, and that their drivers wouldn't man the buses.

On May 15, unable to get bus transportation to their next scheduled stop in Montgomery, Alabama, the riders flew to New Orleans, where they decided to disband without carrying through their original plan to proceed through Montgomery to Mississippi. By then, however, several other groups had begun Freedom Rides of their own. When one bus from Nashville, Tennessee, arrived in Birmingham, the driver refused to take the riders on to Montgomery, and the police took the riders into protective custody.

On May 19 Birmingham Police Commissioner Eugene "Bull" Connor—who was to become known as one of the most rabid segregationist officials in the country—drove the riders in protective custody more than a hundred miles and put them out on a highway at the Alabama-Tennessee border. The message was clear: *Stay out of Birmingham.* But the riders, undaunted, returned immediately to Birmingham for another confrontation. They appeared at a bus terminal and asked for tickets to Montgomery. When they were refused, they sat in at the terminal overnight.

Meanwhile, Alabama officials went into state court and obtained an injunction prohibiting CORE and other civil-rights groups from conducting additional Freedom Rides in the state. But new Freedom Riders, contending that the injunction violated their constitutional rights, continued to pour into Alabama and seek desegregated service at various terminals. On May 20 Alabama Governor John Patterson warned, "We are going to do all we can to enforce the laws of the state on the highways and anywhere else, but we are not going to escort these agitators."

A short time later, Greyhound employees agreed to provide transportation to Montgomery for the riders who had stayed overnight at the terminal and various others. As the bus made its way toward Montgomery, the FBI informed Montgomery police that it understood segregationists planned to attack the riders when they arrived. The police replied that they were confident they could handle the situation, but when the bus pulled into Montgomery, a crowd of about three hundred whites assaulted the riders for almost twenty minutes before enough policemen arrived to halt the violence. Serious injuries were incurred not only by several of the Freedom Riders but also by an administrative assistant from U.S. Attorney General Robert F. Kennedy's office who had ridden the bus as an observer.

The mob action in Montgomery persuaded the Kennedy administration that the time had come for federal action. Attorney General Kennedy announced that he was sending six hundred federal marshals to Montgomery to protect the Freedom Riders and keep the peace. The marshals would be under the command of Deputy Attorney General Byron White (later appointed to the U.S. Supreme Court) and James McShane, the U.S. marshal for the District of Columbia (later appointed the nation's chief marshal).

On May 21 Dr. Martin Luther King, Jr., cut short a speaking tour in the North and flew to Montgomery to address a mass rally at the First Baptist Church. By the time he arrived, about twelve hundred blacks and a smattering of white sympathizers were gathered inside the church. Outside was a mob of white segregationists that eventually numbered about four thousand. The federal marshals ringed the church, trying to keep the increasingly menacing mob from invading the rally. Local and state policemen were also on the scene. While most of the local officers merely stood by and watched, many of the state policemen worked side by side with the federal marshals in an attempt to maintain order. But even with the mutual cooperation of the marshals and the state policemen, the mob was too large to control. Those inside the church felt trapped; there was no way they could safely leave the building. Dr. King telephoned Attorney General Kennedy's office to ask that more manpower be sent immediately to the church. Kennedy telephoned Governor Patterson, saying that unless Patterson took adequate steps to protect the people inside the church, the President would federalize the Alabama National Guard and order Guardsmen to surround the church.

Before reinforcements could arrive, the situation had become far more critical. The angry mob began throwing bricks, bottles, and rocks through the air. Debris smashed the church's stained-glass windows and rained down on those inside. The screaming men and women were on the verge of mass panic. Dr. King tried to calm them. "Let us join hands and sing," he urged. While the onslaught continued, the Freedom Riders and their supporters sang chorus after chorus of "We Shall Overcome."

The marshals used tear gas to drive back the mob, but as the gas drifted away the rioters charged the church again and again. Several times they almost broke through the officers' lines. But the officers somehow held them off until the National Guardsmen arrived. It was morning before the Guardsmen, marshals, and state and local policemen could clear the area of rioters and permit those inside the church to leave.

For two days leaders of the Freedom Rides postponed further action to allow tempers to cool. Although they were employing a strategy of confrontation, they were anxious to avoid additional violence. Meanwhile, more black and white students—plus other sympathizers, such as clergymen and college professors—poured into Montgomery to join the Freedom Rides when they resumed. On May 24, under the protection of National Guardsmen, a contingent of riders appeared at the Trailways depot in Montgomery.

Eleven blacks, including CORE Director James Farmer, and one white sat down at a lunch counter designated "for whites only" and succeeded in being served. This appeared to be a signal victory, since Montgomery had been considered one of the toughest Southern cities to desegregate. (The victory, however, was short-lived. The next day other Freedom Riders served at the same counter were arrested by local police on charges of breaking the peace.)

James Farmer and his contingent of riders boarded a Trailways bus shortly after their stop at the lunch counter, and the bus, escorted by Guardsmen and state policemen, set off for Mississippi. When the bus pulled into the terminal at Jackson, the Mississippi state capital, eight of the black riders walked toward the white-men's toilet. Local policemen politely asked them not to enter. They politely refused to obey, and just as politely were arrested. More arrests followed as busloads of Freedom Riders arrived in Jackson. Most of the defendants were convicted and fined or jailed—setting the stage for appeals that would test the constitutionality of arrests for violation of segregation laws.

All told, more than 1,000 persons took part in various Freedom Rides. The cost of transporting them totaled more than $20,000 and the legal expenses involved in defending them and fighting to desegregate terminals exceeded $300,000.

In the end they achieved their objectives. Many terminal facilities in Southern cities were desegregated. Ultimately the U.S. Supreme Court ruled that most of the arrests of the riders had been unconstitutional. And on November 1, 1961, the Interstate Commerce Commission banned all segregated facilities in terminals.

As in the case of the Montgomery bus boycott, the success of the confrontation strategy in the sit-ins and Freedom

Rides resulted from a combination of factors. Among the most important was the strict discipline displayed by the demonstrators. Their careful training in the philosophy and techniques of nonviolent confrontation prepared them to refrain from retaliating even when provoked. Such restraint and courage brought them a great outpouring of popular support, creating a climate conducive to changing the segregation policies. The responsible tactics of the civil-rights groups generated generally favorable press coverage, further increasing sympathy for their cause.

Another important factor in their success was the demonstrators' pursuit of clearly defined, attainable goals that were obviously justifiable on moral and legal grounds. They did not muddy the waters by making outlandish demands that would be impossible to achieve.

By combining confrontation strategy with resort to the courts, the demonstrators won several important victories. Neither confrontations alone nor lawsuits alone would have gained these broad advances. Only the determined reliance on the dual course could have succeeded.

But beyond their importance in integrating facilities, the sit-in movement and the Freedom Rides provided a new tactic: the sit-in technique itself, which would be used again and again in political confrontations involving a broad range of issues besides segregation.

3
Integrating Southern Universities

NOT all acts of political confrontation were committed by supporters of the civil-rights movement. Many were carried out by angry whites determined to prevent desegregation, even if it meant armed conflict with the forces of government. The most serious confrontation of this sort occurred during the fall of 1962 on the campus of the University of Mississippi, popularly known as Ole Miss.

Despite *Brown v. Board of Education,* the Supreme Court's 1954 decision that opened the way to racial integration of public schools, Ole Miss and numerous other universities, colleges, high schools, junior highs, and elementary schools in various sections of the country remained segregated eight years later. Mississippi in particular stood as a symbolic stronghold of segregation, resisting with determination every effort to integrate its schools. And, of all the schools in the state, Ole Miss represented the strongest bastion of segregation.

In early 1961 a black Mississippian named James Howard Meredith launched an attempt to crack the segregation barrier at Ole Miss. Then twenty-seven, Meredith was an Air Force veteran attending the all-black Jackson State College. Feeling that the education at Ole Miss was superior to that at Jackson State, he applied for admission to the all-white school. When Ole Miss officials learned that Meredith was black, they threw a number of obstacles in his path—for example, they refused to accept his college credits from Jackson State and insisted that they would accept only applicants who could provide character references from six Ole Miss alumni. Meredith pointed out that, as a black, he found it impossible to get six white alumni to supply such references. His application was rejected. Ole Miss officials maintained he was rejected not because of his race, but because he could not meet the usual admission requirements.

With the help of attorneys from the NAACP Legal Defense and Educational Fund, Meredith filed suit in federal court to overturn the university's decision and gain admission. After suffering several legal setbacks, he finally obtained a court order, upheld by the late U.S. Supreme Court Justice Hugo Black, directing Ole Miss officials to accept him for the fall 1962 semester.

At that point, Mississippi Governor Ross Barnett embraced a policy that bordered on the politics of confrontation. Barnett declared an official state policy of defying federal-court desegregation orders, even though he knew the federal government would be obliged to enforce them. The Governor directed state officials to go to jail rather than obey the federal-court orders. In doing so, he invoked the controversial doctrine of interposition. This doctrine, dating back to the Civil War, purported to declare void any federal law that a state determined was usurping the rights reserved to the states. Barnett contended that the operation of public schools was a state responsibility, and that neither the federal government nor the federal courts could tell the states how to run them. Although the United States Supreme Court had previously ruled that interposition was an "illegal defiance of constitutional law," Barnett insisted that he had the right to invoke the doctrine. And many other state officials, plus thousands of white Mississippi citizens, vowed to support his stand against the federal government.

Until then the Kennedy administration had taken no part in the Ole Miss dispute. The fight had been solely between Ole Miss and state officials on one side and James Meredith and his NAACP lawyers on the other. But with Barnett openly pledging to violate the federal-court orders, the administration in Washington had no choice but to enforce the decrees. Accordingly, Attorney General Kennedy announced that federal marshals would be sent to protect Meredith when he tried to enroll at Ole Miss. Kennedy phoned Barnett and assured him there would be no massive show of strength by the federal government; a maximum of five marshals would be assigned to Meredith.

Barnett responded by personally taking over the administration of the university. He persuaded the Ole Miss trustees to designate him acting registrar and give him other powers governing the university. On September 20, 1962, when Meredith showed up to register with four marshals and a small contingent of Justice Department lawyers, he was confronted by about 200 state policemen, a large crowd of students, and Governor Barnett. A university official read a proclamation designating Barnett acting registrar. Barnett then told Meredith that his application had once again been rejected. Meredith and the federal contingent left the campus, serving notice that they would return.

Justice Department attorneys then went into federal court, asking that Barnett and university officials be cited for contempt if they persisted in defying the previous orders to enroll Meredith. At that point, the university trustees decided to bow to the authority of the federal courts, and said they would register Meredith. But Barnett remained adamant, and obtained his own order from a state court forbidding Meredith's registration. Moreover, he issued an executive order directing state police to arrest anyone—including federal officials and marshals—who tried to arrest or fine a state official in connection with the Meredith case. If all the orders given by various officials were to be carried out, the possibility loomed that federal and state officers might try to arrest one another. If one side or another resisted, federal and state law-enforcement officers could wind up in a *High Noon* showdown, facing each other at gunpoint.

On September 25 Meredith appeared at the office of the Ole Miss trustees in Jackson. University Registrar Robert Ellis, who had agreed to enroll Meredith, was waiting for him by prearrangement. But Barnett also showed up, accompanied by various state legislators and about a hundred state policemen, and again stopped the registration.

The following day, back at the Ole Miss campus at Oxford, another attempt was made to register Meredith. This time Meredith, accompanied by five carloads of federal marshals led by Chief Marshal James McShane and Assistant U.S. Attorney General John Doar, was turned back by Lieutenant Governor Paul Johnson, representing Governor Barnett, and a cordon of state policemen.

President John F. Kennedy decided that he could no longer avoid a show of force. He ordered his aides to take the steps necessary to enforce the court orders—even if it meant using military force. He hoped to avoid sending troops to Ole Miss, but he made it clear that he would do so as a last resort. Various military contingents were put on alert, ready to move into Mississippi on short notice. Hundreds of federal marshals from all sections of the country, specially trained for riot-control duty, were ordered to converge on a Naval air station at Memphis, Tennessee, eighty-seven miles from Ole Miss, to prepare for the expected campus showdown.

At the same time, secret negotiations aimed at breaking the stalemate were undertaken by President Kennedy, his brother, and Governor Barnett. The Governor was under heavy pressure from some of Mississippi's leading citizens to back down from his defiant stance, but he desperately wanted to save face with his more rabid segregationist supporters. Several compromises were proposed by Barnett, including one bizarre charade in which Chief Marshal McShane and about twenty-five other marshals would force the Governor at gunpoint to allow Meredith to enter the campus and enroll. The Kennedys, recognizing the potential for violence, rejected the scheme. Ultimately, Barnett agreed to a plan according to which the federal contingent, escorted by state troopers, would bring Meredith onto the campus, secure the area, and enable the black student to enroll. Barnett would not come to the campus. This plan might have worked smoothly if Barnett and/or the Kennedys had made it public in advance, but in order to allow Barnett his face-saving gesture, it was kept secret. Thus, even after surrendering in private to the Kennedys, Barnett continued insisting publicly that he would do everything possible to resist Meredith's enrollment.

In response to the governor's public statements and those of his supporters, hordes of white segregationists swarmed toward Ole Miss from all sections of the country. They intended to place a "wall of flesh"—advocated by many Mississippians—between the campus and the federal marshals. Many of them carried rifles, pistols, and other arms, and they were prepared to use them, if necessary, to drive back the federal men. Although they did not use the term, they were planning a massive exercise in the politics of confrontation.

Meanwhile, President Kennedy federalized the Mississippi National Guard. In addition, almost fourteen hundred regular Army troops with riot-control training were airlifted to the Naval air station in Memphis and placed on standby alert.

The final acts in the confrontation drama were played out on the Ole Miss campus beginning on Sunday, September 30, 1962. Attorney General Kennedy's chief aide, Deputy Attorney General Nicholas de B. Katzenbach (who later succeeded Kennedy as Attorney General), flew in from Washington to take charge of the federal operation. From Jackson, Barnett sent a four-man contingent of state officials to represent him. Large numbers of state policemen and local law-enforcement officers were also on the scene.

On a road between the Oxford airport and the campus, a convoy of six Army trucks carrying the first group of marshals was escorted to the campus by state policemen. A crowd of whites lining the road became increasingly hostile as additional marshals arrived. When a sufficient force was on the scene, the marshals encircled the university's main administration building, the Lyceum. State policemen were stationed at the campus gates, with orders to allow only students, university staff members, and other authorized persons to enter.

Shortly before 7 P.M., a light plane carrying James Meredith landed at the Oxford airport. He was driven to the campus, taken in through a little-used entrance, and escorted to a dormitory where a two-room suite had been set aside for him and the forty-one marshals serving as his immediate bodyguards. The chief bodyguard was a marshal from Florida named Cecil Miller, whose strength, toughness, and courage had earned him the nickname "the James Bond of the U.S. Marshals Service."

Since the main force of marshals was stationed around

the Lyceum, most Ole Miss students assumed Meredith was in that building. A crowd of the white students formed in front of the Lyceum, razzing the marshals, chanting school cheers, and shouting support for Governor Barnett. Meanwhile, for reasons that never were explained, the state policemen at the campus gates relaxed their security, and hundreds of outsiders surged onto the university grounds. As they mingled with the students in front of the Lyceum, the crowd began to turn into a mob. Those in the mob knew nothing of Barnett's secret agreement with the Kennedys, and assumed that the Governor would somehow stave off Meredith's enrollment if they stood firmly behind him.

The first violence on the campus broke out when a television cameraman tried to make his way through the mob. Dozens of men surged around him, beating him and smashing his camera and lights. Minutes later, another television newsman and his wife, driving across the campus in a station wagon, were surrounded by about two hundred persons and severely beaten.

Now the violence began in earnest. A marshal was hit in the face with a large piece of concrete hurled by someone in the mob. Additional chunks of concrete, followed by rocks, bottles, and Molotov cocktails (pop bottles filled with gasoline and ignited with cloth wicks) were thrown at the marshals. Through it all, the marshals stood firm but did not retaliate.

As the situation grew increasingly tense, the marshals asked permission to use tear gas, but Chief Marshal McShane urged them to hold off a while longer. The Army trucks that had brought the marshals to the campus were parked in front of the Lyceum. Suddenly, several hundred demonstrators charged forward and began rocking the trucks from side to side, trying to overturn them. The marshals donned gas masks, but still did not resort to tear gas.

Then an eight-foot length of pipe hurtled out of the mob and struck a marshal in the head. Moments later, a bottle filled with acid struck a marshal and sent the liquid trickling down his arm.

"Fire!" McShane shouted. The marshals, under orders not to use firearms, responded by firing tear-gas cartridges. The tear gas drove the mob back temporarily, but the Lyceum was to be charged countless times throughout the night. What later came to be known as "the Ole Miss riot" was on now in dead earnest. The mob was in a frenzy, and the marshals were left alone to withstand its onslaughts. State police and other Mississippi lawmen, claiming that their gas masks did not protect them against the type of gas being used by the marshals, withdrew from the campus.

A short time later, retired Army General Edwin Walker —who had become a leader of some ultra-conservatives after being disciplined for trying to indoctrinate his troops with John Birch Society propaganda—made an impassioned speech on the campus urging the rioters to continue their protest. The crowd surged toward the line of marshals, heaving rocks, sticks, and bottles. The marshals closed ranks, charged at the rioters, and fired volleys of tear gas. The rioters, choking from the fumes, retreated to a monument honoring soldiers of the Confederacy and listened to a second speech by Walker. They then charged again, but were driven back.

Now the rioters brought firearms into play. Some had pistols, some rifles, some shotguns, some ancient squirrel-hunting guns. Snipers began shooting at the marshals, at federal and university officials standing behind the windows of the Lyceum, at newsmen, at anyone who looked as if he were not on the rioters' side. At about 9:15 P.M. a French reporter named Paul Guihard, covering the confrontation for French and British news agencies, was led to a deserted section of the campus by one or more of the rioters. A .38-caliber pistol was fired once into his back, killing him. Later, a young jukebox repairman named Ray Gunter, who had come to the campus from a nearby town merely to watch the confrontation, was struck in the head by a bullet. He died en route to a hospital, evidently the victim of a stray shot. Many of the marshals also suffered bullet wounds.

The rioters tried to crash into the Lyceum with a bulldozer and a fire engine, but were driven off by the marshals. Several times the marshals requested permission to use firearms against those who were shooting at them, but each time Deputy Attorney General Katzenbach or Chief Marshal McShane urged them to hold off a little longer and rely only on the tear gas to defend themselves.

Eventually a small group of rioters discovered that Meredith was in the dormitory, and tried to rush his suite. Marshal Cecil Miller put Meredith inside a closet, with mattresses all around him to protect him from bullets, and Miller then stood with his back to the door, pistol in hand. He planned to open fire on the first rioter who burst into the room and keep firing until his ammunition was gone. But such drastic action never became necessary. Other marshals stationed outside the dorm drove off the rioters with tear gas, and, for some unexplained reason, word that Meredith was inside the dorm never reached the main body of rioters.

Still the violence continued. Finally, with approval from Washington, Katzenbach ordered a local National Guard contingent of sixty men to enter the campus and help the marshals. The Guardsmen, all Mississippians, and many of them Ole Miss students, did their duty. They marched through the mob, taking both physical and verbal abuse, and fell in with the marshals in front of the Lyceum, but even their aid was insufficient.

In the end President Kennedy was forced to send Army troops to the campus. The soldiers, marshals and Guardsmen, under continuing fire, finally cleared the campus of rioters at about 5 A.M. on Monday. There were additional skirmishes in the town of Oxford, but by 7:45 A.M. the riot was over.

Fifteen minutes later, James Meredith was led into the Lyceum and enrolled. He attended his first classes later in the day. It had taken sixteen months of legal wrangling and an interminable night of bloodshed, but Meredith was now a bona fide Ole Miss student, and would go on to earn his degree.

The cost had been heavy. One hundred eighty marshals —almost half those sent to Ole Miss—had been wounded, twenty-seven by gunfire. Two people were dead. Many others besides the marshals had been wounded. The campus was a shambles. More than three hundred people had been arrested, including General Walker, who was charged with inciting and engaging in "an insurrection against the authority of the United States and the laws thereof." A federal grand jury, however, refused to indict Walker and all but four of the others arrested, and Mississippi trial juries eventually found these four not guilty.

What conclusions can be drawn from the violent confrontation at Ole Miss? Why did the forces bent on provoking the confrontation fail to achieve their goals? Were their acts of confrontation responsible?

The behavior of the white rioters, which led to widespread bloodshed, can be branded only as irresponsible. Part of the secret to the success of earlier confrontation movements, such as the Montgomery bus boycott and the Freedom Rides, had been their nonviolent nature. Although some of the participants had violated local laws as a means of testing them in the courts, they had not caused physical harm to anyone or anything.

Where participants in the earlier confrontations had been highly disciplined, those at Ole Miss were disorganized. Where the earlier participants had set clearly defined, attainable goals, those at Ole Miss made no practical demands. Federal marshals could hardly be expected to surrender James Meredith to a mob that might lynch him. Perhaps most important, the attempt to mount what could be regarded only as an armed insurrection against the United States government surely had no hope of success. No matter what the cost in lives, injuries, and property damage, the government was duty-bound to put down the insurrection.

Governor Barnett and his aides cannot escape their share of the blame for the disaster at Ole Miss. They whipped the people of Mississippi and other states into the frenzy that led to the outburst of violence. The fact that Barnett stayed away from the campus at the time of the final confrontation does not relieve him of heavy responsibility for what happened there. His politically motivated insistence on keeping secret from the public his private surrender to the Kennedy administration led many of the rioters to believe he supported their defiance of the federal forces.

Despite the disastrous confrontation at Ole Miss, the following year the Governor of the neighboring state of Alabama decided to wage a similar battle to prevent the desegregation of the University of Alabama. The Governor, George C. Wallace, had been elected on a promise to keep Alabama's schools segregated. He had pledged: "Segregation now . . . segregation tomorrow . . . segregation forever." And he had vowed to stand personally "in the schoolhouse door" to bar the enforcement of federal-court orders requiring integration of Alabama schools.

As far back as 1956, a black woman named Autherine Lucy had been enrolled briefly at the University of Alabama in Tuscaloosa. But on her third day there rioting students drove her from the campus. After she accused university officials of sharing responsibility for the riot, Miss Lucy was expelled. And for the next seven years no other blacks were enrolled at the university or at any other white school in Alabama.

The segregated system was challenged in 1963 by two blacks—Vivian J. Malone and Jimmy Hood—who filed suit in federal court for admission to the university. A federal judge ruled in their favor and was supported by the appellate courts. University officials made it clear that they were willing to accept the students, but not so Governor Wallace. He served notice that he would go to jail, if necessary, to keep the university segregated.

The potential for violence at the University of Alabama could have been just as great as at Ole Miss. For one thing, Tuscaloosa was a stronghold of the Ku Klux Klan. It was the home of Robert Shelton, Imperial Wizard of the United Klans, who was a staunch backer of Governor Wallace and who was doing everything he could to stir up opposition to the blacks' enrollment. For another, many outsiders swarmed into town for the expected confrontation—just as they had swarmed into Oxford, Mississippi—bent on defying the federal authorities.

But a variety of factors tended to reduce the likelihood of another riot. Governor Wallace, while shouting his defiance of the courts and the Kennedys, urged his followers to let him make his stand on their behalf. Local police moved effectively to maintain tight control of the campus and the city. State police, although under the command of a gruff segregationist named Albert J. Lingo, agreed to cooperate with local officers and federal marshals in keeping the peace. Thus, when the showdown came, on June 11, 1963, it appeared it would be between Wallace and the federal men, with outsiders acting only as bystanders.

The Kennedy administration had learned in the Ole Miss riot that reluctance to commit military forces early in a confrontation could prove costly. Had the Army troops moved to the Ole Miss campus sooner, some of the bloodshed undoubtedly could have been prevented. Thus, for the Tuscaloosa showdown President Kennedy was prepared to use troops if there was any sign of armed resistance. Army General Creighton Abrams (who is Army Chief of Staff at this writing) was sent to Tuscaloosa in advance to direct any military operations that might become necessary. Meanwhile, a familiar cast of characters arrived to head the federal government's civilian operations. Among those on the scene were Deputy Attorney General Katzenbach, who again was in charge of the federal contingent, Chief Marshal McShane, and Deputy Marshal Cecil Miller.

In response to Governor Wallace's repeated statements that he would stand "in the schoolhouse door," President Kennedy issued a proclamation accusing the Governor of entering with others into an "unlawful obstruction and combination" to defy the federal courts, and he ordered the Governor "to cease and desist." But Wallace refused to obey, insisting he would make his stand.

Less than two hours after Kennedy issued the proclamation, a car carrying the two black students pulled up in front of the university building where registration was to take place. The students, accompanied by Justice Department lawyers and a small contingent of marshals, remained in the car. Deputy Attorney General Katzenbach walked toward the building. Waiting for him "in the schoolhouse door" was Governor Wallace, surrounded by aides and state troopers. The confrontation was at hand.

Katzenbach approached Wallace and told him he had a copy of the President's proclamation, "commanding" the governor to cease and desist from blocking the implementation of the court orders. But Wallace, holding up his hand as if he were a traffic cop, said he had a proclamation of his own. He then read a five-page statement into a microphone that carried his words to the large crowd gathered on the campus, and to television and radio equipment set up nearby.

"I stand here today as Governor of this sovereign state and refuse to willingly submit to illegal usurpation of power by the central government," Wallace said. "My action does not constitute disobedience to legislative and constitutional provisions. It is not defiance for defiance['s] sake, but for the purpose of raising basic and fundamental constitutional questions. . . . I stand before you today in place of thousands of other Alabamans whose presence would have confronted you had I been derelict and neglected to fulfill the obligations of my office. . . ."

When Wallace finished his statement, Katzenbach said, "Governor Wallace, I take it from that statement that you are going to stand in the door and that you are not going to carry out the orders of the court and that you are going to resist us from doing so. Is that correct?"

Wallace replied, "I stand according to my statement."

Katzenbach scowled. "Governor, I am not interested in a show," he said. ". . . I am interested in the orders of these courts being enforced. . . . I would ask you once again to responsibly stand aside. . . . From the outset, Governor, all of us have known that the final chapter of this history will be the admission of these students. These students will remain on this campus. They will register today. They will go to school tomorrow."

Wallace neither moved from the doorway nor made any

reply. He simply stood there, with his shoulders thrown back stiffly and his lips taut. In accordance with a prearranged federal plan, Katzenbach walked away. If at all possible, President Kennedy and his aides wanted to avoid being forced to arrest the Governor. An arrest, they felt, would create unnecessary discord among Southern citizens and play into Wallace's hands—in effect making him a martyr and giving him fresh political ammunition. Thus, the federal plan so far had not allowed for Wallace to block the students and thereby place himself in contempt of court. Since the students had remained in the car, Wallace had not blocked them, only Katzenbach.

After Katzenbach had withdrawn from the building, he and the federal contingent escorted the black students to two dormitories. University officials, who had long expressed willingness to accept the students, and had urged Wallace to avoid the campus confrontation, assigned Hood and Miss Malone to dormitory rooms, even though they had not yet registered.

While Hood and Miss Malone waited in the dorms, President Kennedy federalized the Alabama National Guard. A National Guard general, Henry Graham, flew to Tuscaloosa and took command of the local Guard contingent. He then met with Army General Abrams, other federal officials, and several of Governor Wallace's advisers. The federal plan called for Graham to approach the doorway with a few Guardsmen, all local men, and tell Wallace that he had orders to remove the Governor. All concerned agreed that force would be used only as a last resort—that Wallace would be given every chance to withdraw under his own power.

About 3:30 P.M., not quite five hours after the original doorway confrontation, General Graham and four National Guardsmen walked up to the doorway to face the Governor.

When they reached a point a few yards from Wallace, Graham snapped to attention and asked the Governor to step aside. Wallace pulled a rumpled piece of paper from his pocket and said he wanted to make another statement. Graham allowed him to do so. "I am grateful to the people of Alabama for the restraint which they have shown," Wallace said. "I ask the people of Alabama to remain calm, to help us in this fight. We must have no violence. . . . The Guardsmen are our brothers. The trend toward military dictatorship continues. But this is a constitutional fight, and we are winning."

Despite his last words of bravado, Wallace had lost, and he knew it. He snapped to attention, threw General Graham a salute, received one in return, and stepped from the doorway. A short time later he left the campus, and the black students were registered. Two days later another black, Dave McGlathery, was enrolled without incident at the University of Alabama branch in Huntsville. Wallace, who had vowed to stand in every schoolhouse door in the state, did not even show up. He knew it would be futile. The desegregation of the University of Alabama marked a milestone in the black revolution; it meant that at least token desegregation had been accomplished in the public schools of all fifty states.

Wallace's claim that he made the doorway stand because the courts had not considered the constitutional issues in the dispute seems frivolous. The courts had deliberated on the issues, and had repeatedly ruled against Wallace's position. He could not be blamed for disliking those decisions, but as a lawyer, a former judge, and the head of a state government, he could justifiably be accused of encouraging lawlessness by pledging to defy court orders. Given the outcome of the Ole Miss affair and other recent events, Wallace must have known that his effort was doomed to failure and that the confrontation would end with the enrollment of the black students. Thus, his insistence on going through with the doorway episode seems no more than a hollow gesture, aimed at boosting Wallace's political stock among segregationists. It could have ended in tragic violence. Fortunately, it did not. But, along with the Ole Miss riot, it demonstrates that such tactics should not be adopted frivolously.

The politics of confrontation, when practiced judiciously, can be extremely effective. When practiced irresponsibly, they can not only prove disastrous; they can rarely succeed.

4

Riots and Reform

WHILE the effort to desegregate Southern universities progressed, the black revolution proceeded on other fronts in both the South and the North. Acts of political confrontation continued to play a prominent role.

One of the main battlegrounds was Birmingham, Alabama. Between 1957 and 1963, the city was the scene of at least eighteen bombings directed against black activists and their sympathizers. The Ku Klux Klan had burned more than fifty crosses as warnings against continued desegregation efforts. Despite steps toward integration taken elsewhere in the South, Birmingham clung stubbornly to its segregation policy. Schools, restaurants, lunch counters, rest rooms, drinking fountains, and department-store fitting rooms all were rigidly segregated. The city had closed its public parks rather than comply with a federal court's integration order.

Birmingham's symbolic segregationist leader was Eugene "Bull" Connor, whose elected position as city's public-safety commissioner placed him in charge of both the police and fire departments. Connor was a powerful political figure. Under his direction, Birmingham police had long maintained a "get-tough" policy with civil-rights activists. Demonstrators had been hauled off to jail at the slightest provocation. The police had even arrested a white United States senator who, while in Birmingham to deliver a speech, had walked through a door marked "colored." Connor had vowed to defy the U.S. Supreme Court, and had offered to wage a fist fight, if necessary, with Attorney General Robert Kennedy. And he had predicted that "blood will run in the streets" of Birmingham before he would allow it to be integrated.

In the spring of 1963, Dr. Martin Luther King, Jr., led a task force of civil-rights leaders into Birmingham to mobilize local blacks for a series of confrontations with Connor's segregation policies. As in previous confrontations, Dr. King and his associates set well-defined goals for the Birmingham campaign. Their demands included desegregation in major stores of lunch counters, rest rooms, fitting rooms, and drinking fountains; upgrading and nondiscriminatory hiring of blacks throughout the city's business and industrial community; and creation of a biracial citizens' committee to try to iron out problems between the races.

Arriving in the city with his task force, King described Birmingham as "the most thoroughly segregated big city in the United States today." He said he planned to lead demonstrations until "Pharaoh lets God's people go." The demonstrations began on a small scale. Small groups of blacks showed up at downtown stores, intending to sit in at the segregated lunch counters if they were not served. Merchants responded by quietly closing the counters or calling the police, who made routine arrests. At first matters seemed relatively calm. But as the demonstrations continued day after day, tensions rose.

Bull Connor went into State Circuit Court and obtained an injunction barring any further racial demonstrations. King, contending that the injunction violated the demonstrators' constitutional right to assemble peaceably, announced that he and his followers would ignore it. In his first major act of political confrontation in Birmingham, King then led about a thousand demonstrators on a march toward the business district, in defiance of the injunction. As a result, King and various other demonstrators were arrested and jailed. Although he could have posted bail, King elected to remain in jail to dramatize the protest.

During the demonstrations, eight of Birmingham's leading white clergymen—Protestant, Catholic, and Jewish—issued a statement calling the protests "unwise and untimely." From his jail cell, King wrote a lengthy reply that received wide attention under the title "A Letter from the Birmingham Jail." "You deplore the demonstrations . . . taking place in Birmingham," he wrote. "But . . . your statement, I am sorry to say, fails to express a similar concern for the conditions that brought the demonstrations into being. . . . Oppressed people cannot remain oppressed forever. The urge for freedom will eventually come. . . . Recognizing this vital urge that has engulfed the Negro community, one should readily understand public demonstrations. The Negro has many pent-up resentments and latent frustrations. He has to get them out. . . . I have no fear about the outcome of our struggle in Birmingham and all over the nation because the goal of America is freedom. We will win our freedom because the sacred heritage of our nation and the eternal will of God are embodied in our echoing demands."

After serving a five-day jail sentence, King was released, and secret negotiations aimed at settling the dispute were begun. Participating on one side were members of a subcommittee of the Birmingham Chamber of Commerce, and on the other side prominent Birmingham blacks, aides of Dr. King, and eventually King himself.

Meanwhile, the demonstrations continued, and the atmosphere on the streets grew increasingly volatile. On May 3 violence erupted when a large group of demonstrators gathered at a park in the black business district. Bull Connor spread policemen and firemen, backed by snarling police dogs, through the park to break up what he considered an illegal demonstration. Suddenly, a black boy shouted, "Freedom! Get the white dogs!" Connor ordered: "Let 'em have it."

The firemen turned on high-pressure hoses and used the rushing sprays of water to knock demonstrators to the ground or against trees. The police dogs lunged at protesters, biting many blacks, including three children. The demonstrators remained orderly, following the nonviolence doctrine. But other blacks in the park started throwing rocks at the policemen and firemen. A rain of bricks and bottles fell on the officers from the roof of a nearby building. Several officers and a newsman were injured. Gradually the fire hoses wore down the rioting blacks, and they dispersed.

When there was a similar outbreak the next day, King's aides, realizing the immense potential for violence, called off a scheduled demonstration. The two eruptions focused national attention on the Birmingham confrontations, and Attorney General Kennedy sent Burke Marshall, chief of the Justice Department's Civil Rights Division, to Birmingham to try to bring about a settlement between the black and white negotiators. But the negotiating process was slow, and while it continued, so did the demonstrations—resulting in a total of 2,400 arrests since the beginning of the campaign.

The heightened tensions increased the pressure on the white negotiators to settle the crisis. Birmingham's national image was taking a nose dive. Local blacks were boycotting white-owned stores, so merchants were hard pressed financially. Officials of national corporations with Birmingham plants—such as United States Steel Corporation, the city's largest employer—were pressuring their local executives to end the dispute.

Finally, on May 10, the white businessmen and the black leaders reached an agreement. Its terms were the following: The desegregation of lunch counters, rest rooms, fitting rooms, and drinking fountains in the city's major stores would begin within ninety days. The upgrading and nondiscriminatory hiring of blacks throughout Birmingham's industrial community would begin within sixty days. All persons arrested during demonstrations would be released on bail. And there would be continuing discussions between black and white leaders to resolve any further problems that arose. Dr. King and his aides agreed to halt the demonstrations, but did not rule out resuming them if the terms of the agreement were not fulfilled.

In revealing the agreement, King said, "I am very happy to be able to announce that we have come today to the climax of a long struggle for justice, freedom, and human dignity in the city of Birmingham. I say the climax and not the end, for though we have come a long way, there is still a strenuous path before us, and some of it is yet uncharted."

Those words proved to be prophetic. Many in Birmingham, including Bull Connor, denounced the agreement and urged whites to boycott the stores that had agreed to desegregate. Among others adamantly opposed to the agreement were members of the Ku Klux Klan, who conducted a mass rally to demonstrate their displeasure. About a thousand robed Klansmen attended the rally and two crosses were burned.

About a half hour after the rally ended two bombs were thrown at the home of Dr. King's brother, the Reverend A. D. King, pastor of a black Baptist church in Birmingham.

Although nobody was hurt, the explosions left the house a shambles. A short time later another bomb went off at the motel that had served as Dr. King's headquarters in Birmingham.

In the wake of the bombings, hundreds of blacks surged out of taverns, pool halls, night clubs, and small grocery stores in the area and went on a rampage, attacking policemen and firemen who arrived on the scene, setting fire to white-owned buildings, and shouting that they would stand for no more oppression by whites. By and large, these blacks were not members of the protest movement. Leaders of the movement tried to persuade them to halt the violence, but with little success. The riot raged for more than four hours. Only when the Reverend A. D. King arrived and pleaded with the mob did the blacks disperse.

At the riot's end, more than fifty persons were being treated in hospitals, and the neighborhood where the riot had started was in ruins. Many people felt that the bombings and the resulting emotional outburst of violence would kill the biracial agreement. But when Dr. King returned to Birmingham the next day, he took a contrary view. "I do not feel the events of last night nullified the agreement at all," he said. "I do not think the bombings were perpetrated or even sanctioned by the majority of white people in Birmingham." And the white businessmen who had negotiated the agreement remained firm in their commitment. Despite temporary setbacks, the agreement took effect, marking another milestone in the history of the confrontation politics practiced by Dr. King.

Dr. King's victory in Birmingham inspired other civil-rights protests in both the North and South. In Jackson, Mississippi, for example, the NAACP led picket-line demonstrations and boycotts, seeking desegregation of rest rooms, restaurants, lunch rooms, theaters, schools, parks, playgrounds, libraries, and other public facilities; equal employment opportunities for blacks; elimination of discriminatory business practices; and creation of a biracial committee to help achieve these goals.

The drive in Jackson was headed by Medgar Evers, Mississippi field secretary for the NAACP. On June 12, 1963, as he returned home late at night after working, Evers was shot to death by a sniper. A militant white segregationist, Byron De La Beckwith, was charged with the murder, but was eventually released when a series of juries could not agree on a verdict. As had been the case in Birmingham following the bombings, rioting by blacks erupted after Evers's murder. It was halted before there were serious injuries or property damage.

Evers's brother, Charles, took over the NAACP job and continued pressing the desegregation demands. In the end, the blacks' confrontation strategy paid off when white community leaders agreed to grant many of the demands. Charles Evers went on to become the first black mayor of Fayette, Mississippi, and one of the most influential black politicians in the country.

In Northern cities such as New York, where there were no segregation laws on the books, frequent instances of discrimination against blacks nonetheless occurred. And civil-rights groups, using the confrontation techniques developed in the South, mounted numerous demonstrations against such discrimination. The targets of many of these demonstrations were huge construction projects—including apartment-house developments and state hospitals—where, protesters claimed, blacks had been denied jobs. Contracting firms maintained that they had no control over who was hired—that their employees came to them through labor-union apprenticeship programs. But black demonstrators, supported by many whites, asserted that they had trouble getting into the apprenticeship programs and were discriminated against even if they did gain entry.

To press their demands for hiring of blacks, the demonstrators in New York and other Northern cities used such confrontation tactics as lying down in the streets to prevent trucks from entering construction sites, picketing these sites to discourage construction workers from reporting for work, and chaining themselves to giant cranes to keep the cranes from being used. As in the South, many demonstrators were arrested. But, also as in the South, their tactics ultimately paid dividends. Agreements were reached to increase substantially the number of blacks accepted into construction unions and apprenticeship programs.

Significantly, confrontation tactics aimed at inappropriate targets produced no tangible results. For example, CORE mounted a demonstration in New York City to protest the fact that a new Harlem public school, attended solely by black and Puerto Rican students, was segregated because of housing patterns. The demonstrators blocked traffic on the Triborough Bridge. The bridge had no relevance to the school dispute. Although the demonstration attracted publicity, it produced no tangible benefits for the protesters' cause.

On a more positive note, the civil-rights ferment throughout the United States resulted in the March on Washington on August 28, 1963. More than two hundred thousand whites and blacks from across the country gathered near the Lincoln Memorial to demonstrate their commitment to the cause of equality for all Americans. Strictly speaking, the march was not an example of confrontation politics, although many observers had expected it to be. Had there been official resistance to the march by the federal government or substantial attempts by those outside the government to prevent it, there might well have been a massive confrontation in Washington. But the government cooperated with the marchers and prevented opponents of the demonstration, such as the Ku Klux Klan, from disrupting it. The main focus of the mass rally—at which Dr. Martin Luther King, Jr., made his famous "I have a dream" speech—was on passage of federal legislation to abolish segregation.

Two months earlier President Kennedy had proposed the most far-reaching civil-rights measure since the Civil War. Among its major provisions was a section outlawing segregation in hotels, restaurants, theaters, and other places of public accommodation. The bill represented Kennedy's direct response to the grievances expressed by civil-rights groups in their campaigns of confrontation. But, as broad as the bill was, it still fell short of satisfying civil-rights leaders' demands. For one thing, it did not contain a provision requiring fair-employment practices—that is, nondiscriminatory hiring, promotion, and wage policies by employers. For another, it did not include a section giving the federal government power to intervene in civil-rights cases on behalf of those who claimed they were the victims of discrimination. Moreover, the climate on Capitol Hill did not seem particularly receptive to the civil-rights bill. President Kennedy was having general problems with Congress, and many Congressmen were antagonized by the confrontation tactics adopted by civil-rights groups.

The March on Washington, followed by additional demonstrations in other cities, was intended to keep the pressure on and assure the bill's passage. But by the time of his assassination on November 22, 1963, President Kennedy had not succeeded in getting the measure through Congress.

When Lyndon B. Johnson succeeded Kennedy as President, he made the bill's passage one of his chief priorities. Johnson argued forcefully that there could be no more fitting memorial to Kennedy than enactment of the sweeping legislation. In the climate of shock and sorrow following the assassination, with Congress anxious to heal the nation's wounds, Johnson was even able to include provisions for fair-employment practices and federal intervention in civil-rights cases. The bill became law in 1964.

While many observers feel that the bill would not have been passed had it not been for Kennedy's murder, it is fair to say that the politics of confrontation played a major role in setting the stage for the Civil Rights Act of 1964.

As effective as it was in opening places of public accommodation to blacks, the Civil Rights Act of 1964 did nothing to halt discriminatory voting practices in the South. White voting registrars in many areas of the South regularly used a variety of technical excuses to prevent blacks from registering to vote. After the passage of the 1964 law, the civil-rights movement shifted its main focus to voting-rights drives. Confrontation tactics such as mass marches and protest rallies were integral parts of these drives.

One of the chief targets was Selma, Alabama, where Dr. King headed a series of confrontations against white authorities led by Sheriff Jim Clark. Within seven weeks, more than two thousand demonstrators—including Dr. King— were in Selma jails. When civil-rights workers organized a protest march from Selma to Montgomery, the potential for violence was so great that President Johnson assigned National Guardsmen, regular Army troops, and federal marshals to protect the marchers. Although the march itself was completed without violence, a white civil-rights worker named Mrs. Viola Liuzzo was shot to death by Ku Klux Klan night-riders while driving back from Montgomery to Selma with a young black man.

The persistence of the civil-rights workers and the recalcitrance of many white Southern officials influenced President Johnson to order the Justice Department to draft a strong new voting-rights bill. With Johnson's firm backing, the bill was passed by Congress and became the Voting Rights Act of 1965. It provided for assignment of federal registrars to areas where local registrars had denied blacks the vote. Under the new law, many thousands of blacks were enabled to vote for the first time.

The confrontation strategy employed in such places as Birmingham, Jackson, and Selma served as an important catalyst for change in this country. All evidence indicates that the white leaders in cities such as Birmingham would have continued to forestall desegregation had it not been for the demonstrations, economic pressures, and publicity generated by the civil-rights movement's confrontation strategy. Similarly, it seems unlikely that the Civil Rights Act of 1964 and the Voting Rights Act of 1965 would have been passed by Congress if the issues had not been dramatized by repeated use of confrontation tactics.

To those who questioned the use of such tactics, Dr. Martin Luther King, Jr., replied: "Nonviolence comes in as the ultimate form of persuasion. It is the method which seeks to implement the just law by appealing to the conscience of the great decent majority who through blindness, fear, pride, or irrationality have allowed their consciences to sleep. The nonviolent resisters can summarize their message in the following simple terms: We will take direct action against injustice without waiting for other agencies to act. We will not obey unjust laws or submit to unjust practices. We will do this peacefully, openly, cheerfully because our aim is to persuade. We adopt the means of nonviolence because our end is a community at peace with itself. We will try to persuade with our words, but if our words fail we will try to persuade with our acts. We will always be willing to talk and seek fair compromise, but we are ready to suffer when necessary and even risk our lives to become witnesses to the truth as we see it."

As previously pointed out, the tactics employed in the black revolution opened the way for the practice of confrontation politics on behalf of a wide range of issues besides civil rights. Succeeding chapters will describe how these tactics were adopted and adapted by groups seeking many kinds of social and political change in America.

II
Rebellion on the Campus

5

Berkeley's Free Speech Movement

WHAT has come to be known as "the campus rebellion" is in large part traceable to the confrontation politics of the black revolution. For one thing, the civil-rights movement awakened the aspirations of many students for greater control over their own destinies. If blacks no longer had to accept the degradation of past years, they reasoned, why shouldn't students be granted parallel "pieces of the action" on the campuses they inhabit? Why shouldn't they have greater freedom of political expression, more voice in how their schools are run, more control over what courses are offered and how they are taught?

Moreover, the students of all races who took part in the civil-rights movement, sympathized with it or merely marveled at its success realized the potential of confrontation strategy.

Thus, it was natural for students to rely on the confrontation tactics developed in the civil-rights movement when they decided the time had come for protest on other issues.

The first major campus rebellion—the one that set the stage for many others—occurred in 1964 at the University of California campus at Berkeley. Many experts feel that the events at Berkeley bore great significance beyond the sphere of confrontation politics; that they represented an enormously important turning point in this country's education process. Three years after the first confrontation at Berkeley, for example, a book entitled *The College Scene Now*, published by the influential newspaper *The National Observer*, had this to say:

> The most important single event in the modern history of American higher education was the student revolution on the Berkeley campus of the University of California. . . . It is a measure of its importance that such a short time has passed and so much has happened that is directly attributable to what happened there. Perhaps it cannot be said that every college and university has been affected. Yet it might be said that any schools not affected can barely claim to be institutions of higher learning. . . . What has happened since Berkeley is that students have become involved as never before in how their schools are run. They are not only showing concern but seeking responsibility in such areas as undergraduate teaching, participation in political and civic activities, curriculum decisions, promotion and tenure policies for the faculty.

What happened at Berkeley? How did it affect the history of confrontation politics? And why did it have such significant impact on American education?

By tradition a sidewalk area near the main entrance to the Berkeley campus had been set aside for the use of various student organizations. Students congregated there to deliver and hear speeches on political and social issues, recruit members for their organizations, raise funds, distribute literature, and carry on a myriad of other activities. It had long been assumed that the sidewalk area was city property, and therefore outside the jurisdiction of university officials. But in September 1964 the university learned that the area actually belonged to the university. As a result, the university administration decided that the rules rigidly controlling political activities elsewhere on the campus would henceforth apply also to the sidewalk area.

The Dean of Students, Katherine Towle, notified all student organizations that they could no longer use the area for their activities. Many students interpreted the decision as an attempt to stifle dissent, since the area had become the hub of various political movements from radical to conservative. Three days after Dean Towle issued her edict, student organizations representing the entire political spectrum formed a coalition to oppose the ban. The coalition asked to meet with Dean Towle and other university officials.

At the meeting Dean Towle made a partial concession. She ruled that students could set up information tables and distribute literature in the area, but they could not use it for speeches and other political activity. The concession did not satisfy the coalition, and it conducted a mass rally on the steps of the university administration building in protest of what it described as arbitrary curbs on students' freedom of speech.

A week later, University Chancellor Edward Strong conceded students the right to campaign for candidates and ballot propositions in the sidewalk area, but continued to forbid its use for other political activities. Other university officials warned that students who engaged in "illegal politics," as defined by the university administration, would be subject to expulsion. Despite the warning, several campus groups refused to abide by the new restrictions.

On September 30, two and a half weeks after Dean Towle's initial edict, the university accused five students of violating the new rules and ordered them to appear before the deans for a disciplinary hearing. In response, more than four hundred students signed written declarations that they had been just as responsible as their five colleagues for the purported breaking of the rules. The four hundred appeared at the administration building, demanding that they also be given disciplinary hearings. All except three of them were barred from the deans' offices. These three, who described themselves as leaders of the four hundred, were added to the original five students subject to disciplinary proceedings. The remaining students demonstrated in protest of both the deans' refusal to see them and the attempt to punish their colleagues. With hundreds of other students joining the protest, the deans called off the hearings—but Chancellor Strong announced that the eight students were suspended indefinitely. That news caused still further protest, and the demonstrating students, adopting the confrontation tactics of the civil-rights movement, sat in peacefully all night at the administration building.

Two days later, in violation of the campus rules, students representing various organizations set up tables for the distributing of literature and other activities on the steps of the administration building. Police were called to break up the unauthorized activities. They arrested one student, Jack Weinberg, who had been manning a table for the campus branch of CORE. But when they tried to take Weinberg away in a patrol car, swarms of students blocked its passage, and forced Weinberg's temporary release.

A short time later, again in violation of the rules, a mass rally was conducted to protest the new regulations. After the rally, which was attended by about two thousand students, many of the protesters surged into the administration building and launched another sit-in. Attempts by faculty members to mediate the dispute were unsuccessful, largely because the administration refused to negotiate on the regulations. The demonstrators continued their sit-in overnight.

In the morning the administration asked the police to send a large force to the campus—prepared to arrest the demonstrators, if necessary. Several hundred policemen came to the campus and surrounded the demonstrators, but held off on making arrests while student leaders met with university officials and faculty members. The university president, Clark Kerr, entered the discussion with the student leaders for the first time. Out of the meeting came an agreement: criminal charges against student Weinberg would be dropped, the police would leave without making further arrests, and the sit-in would end.

The agreement was merely a stopgap solution. It left unresolved the basic dispute over the restrictions on the students' political activities. In an attempt to bridge the gap between the two sides, the university agreed to create the Campus Committee on Political Activity, which was to suggest long-range solutions. Chancellor Strong appointed ten members to the committee. The student coalition was given the right to name two members.

Meanwhile, the coalition had evolved into an organization known as the Free Speech Movement, which included representatives of virtually all campus political, civic, and religious groups. A firebrand student leader named Mario Savio—who was to become a nationally known symbol of campus rebellion—emerged as the chief spokesman for the movement. Under pressure from Savio and other student leaders, the administration agreed to give the Movement the right to name an additional two members to the Campus Committee on Political Activity. Even so, many students complained that the Committee was unfairly stacked against them.

Although the administration ultimately agreed to give the students additional representation, it soon became clear that the committee could not operate effectively. Members reached a stalemate on the issue of whether the university could discipline students and organizations for activities that led to purported "unlawful acts" outside the campus. The campus restrictions remained in effect. In protest, the Free Speech Movement ended its six-week moratorium on challenges to the rules, and various organizations resumed setting up tables on the campus. The administration responded by abolishing the Campus Committee on Political Activity.

Next, a faculty committee recommended that six of the eight students indefinitely suspended on September 30 be reinstated immediately and that the suspensions of the other two, Mario Savio and Arthur Goldberg, be limited to six weeks. The administration refused to act on the recommendation. The university regents then upheld the administration's decision to suspend the eight students and to place Savio and Goldberg on probation for the following semester. The regents also softened the regulations on campus activities somewhat, but still insisted that students and their organizations could be disciplined for supposed "illegal advocacy" of various causes.

Three days later the Free Speech Movement led a confrontation in which more than three hundred students sat in at the administration building to protest the university's discipline policies. Savio and Goldberg were then threatened with additional disciplinary action. In response, the Movement warned that it planned massive demonstrations, and junior faculty members threatened to strike.

On December 2, the Movement sponsored a rally that attracted thousands of students to the area outside the administration building. Later, more than a thousand students surged into the building and began another sit-in. Many remained in the building at nightfall. Early the next day, when the students refused repeated requests to leave the building, California Governor Edmund G. ("Pat") Brown ordered police onto the campus to arrest them. More than eight hundred students were taken into custody, precipitating the greatest crisis in the dispute to that point. While the arrests were being made, graduate students and faculty members picketed campus buildings, protesting the decision to call in the police. A bail fund raised by the faculty was used to gain the release of the arrested students. Amid all this turmoil, a campuswide strike was called, and most classes did not meet for several days.

On December 7, a highly unusual meeting of students, faculty members, and administrators took place. It was addressed by President Kerr and Professor Robert Scalapino, chairman of a committee of university department heads, who outlined proposals for ending the crisis. When Mario Savio tried to address the meeting, police seized him and removed him from the hall. But student protests persuaded the administrators to get Savio released and allow him to speak. In his talk Savio denounced Kerr's proposals as inadequate, and the meeting broke up in disagreement.

It was not until early January 1965 that the crisis was resolved. The university regents, convinced that new leadership was necessary to restore normalcy to the campus, named Martin Meyerson, previously dean of the College of Environmental Design at Berkeley, as acting chancellor to replace Edward Strong. Meyerson, anxious to end the crisis, immediately announced new rules permitting students to set up tables on the steps of the administration building, distribute literature, recruit members for their organizations, raise funds, make speeches, and otherwise engage in political activities, subject only to minor restrictions.

Although Chancellor Meyerson's announcement did not appear very dramatic, it marked a significant victory in the history of confrontation politics. The confrontations at

Berkeley set the stage for the whole era of campus rebellion. Students across the country, and in foreign nations as well, learned from the events at Berkeley that confrontation politics could be used effectively to overturn long-entrenched campus policies.

One reason for the success of the confrontation strategy at Berkeley was that the demonstrations were extremely well-organized. Although the groups making up the Free Speech Movement had diverse philosophies and interests, they all worked together effectively toward their common goals. The protesters' demands were reasonable, and seemed to have the force of moral and legal right behind them. Moreover, the demonstrations were aimed at appropriate targets: at university officials who clearly had the power to effect reforms. Largely for these reasons, the protesters received important support from faculty members, segments of the news media, and the public at large. All these factors combined to contribute to the Movement's success.

Confrontations on the Berkeley campus did not end with Chancellor Meyerson's agreement to loosen the restrictions on political activity. Over the years since 1965, students have demonstrated on a variety of issues. (In fact, the guides on sightseeing buses that pass the campus daily still tell tourists, "At the main campus of the University of California, here in Berkeley, they probably have more demonstrations than at any other campus in the world.")

Meanwhile, the ferment generated by campus confrontations led many Berkeley students to involve themselves more deeply in local politics. With backing from campus radicals, a slate of radical candidates won four seats on the Berkeley City Council. One of the four councilmen, Warren Widener, was chosen as the city's mayor. Although

Widener later split with his fellow radicals on some issues, the radicals' influence on government remained clear. Among the programs pushed through by the radicals were increased hiring of blacks and women by the city and reform of the police department.

In the final analysis, what was perhaps most significant was not the effect of the campus rebellion on Berkeley itself but the example set there for students on hundreds of other campuses.

6

Coast-to-Coast Upheaval

IN THE aftermath of the Berkeley crisis, debates raged at colleges throughout the country over the validity of confrontation politics as a means of changing campus policies. Many argued that the type of demonstrations conducted at Berkeley have no place in an academic community. But others contended that less dramatic means of seeking campus reform had proved unsuccessful and that colleges and universities should not be immune from pressure tactics used elsewhere.

No matter which view was more valid, campus after campus from coast to coast was swept with a wave of political confrontations in the years following the Berkeley rebellion. The student complaints varied widely. Some seemed justified, others capricious. Some demonstrations seemed within the bounds of responsible protest, others far outside those bounds. As the strategy of confrontation politics took hold on the nation's campuses, the disruption was so great that at one point no fewer than 760 universities and colleges either closed down temporarily or seriously considered doing so.

It would obviously be impractical to review here all or

even most of those disruptions, but a brief examination of some of them provides an idea of the range of the protests and issues. It should be kept in mind that for every example of confrontation politics discussed here, there were hundreds of others that followed similar patterns. And, although many of those that are not discussed may have seemed lacking in the drama and significance that attract national attention, they all contributed to the climate that generated a continuing adoption of confrontation politics by diverse groups.

Many of the campus confrontations were, in a sense, extensions of the civil-rights movement. Often, black students—usually supported by at least some of their white colleagues—demonstrated on behalf of projects to make their schools more black-oriented. At the University of Wisconsin, for example, black students went on strike to support their demands for enrollment of more blacks, hiring of more black teachers, establishment of a program that would grant degrees in black studies, the power to hire and fire the teachers and administrators involved in the proposed program, and a guarantee of freedom from punishment for campus demonstrators.

University officials contended they were trying to improve the black-studies program and increase black enrollment, but that some of the students' demands were impractical and that amnesty for all demonstrators was out of the question. In response, many white students joined the strike, and, in defiance of police orders, about fifteen hundred students picketed campus buildings and tried to disrupt classes. Demonstrations continued for a week, with numerous skirmishes between the police and students who tried to enter campus buildings to persuade others to join the strike. Finally, Governor Warren P. Knowles ordered several hundred National Guardsmen to the campus to maintain order.

The Guardsmen, who arrived in jeeps mounted with machine guns, fanned across the campus with fixed bayonets and dispersed the demonstrators. Further acts of confrontation followed. Although the striking students did not win all their demands, the university eventually moved to satisfy many of them.

Similar disorders erupted at Cornell University, the City College of New York, Duke University, Harvard, Notre Dame, the University of Chicago, the State University of New York at Stony Brook, and countless other colleges.

In addition, there were disorders on many predominantly black campuses. One of the most serious of these occurred at South Carolina State College in Orangeburg when black students launched a series of demonstrations over the refusal of a local bowling alley to admit blacks. One night, when policemen came to break up a particularly violent demonstration, the protesters threw firebombs, rocks, and other objects at them. Police contended, but could not prove conclusively, that one or more snipers fired shots at them during the confrontation. When a crowd of students advanced on the officers, the police opened fire and sprayed the crowd with a heavy barrage of bullets and buckshot. When the shooting ended, three students were dead and twenty-seven others were wounded. (Federal prosecutors later obtained an indictment charging nine of the policemen with violating the demonstrators' civil rights by using excessive force, but a jury found the officers not guilty.)

One catalyst for the rising tide of political confrontation on campus was the emergence of the New Left movement. The movement consisted of a multitude of activist organizations ranging from the moderately liberal to the socialist to the communist. On many campuses, the confrontation strategy of small New Left groups attracted support from numerous unaffiliated students. It has been charged, with what appears to be some justification, that militant organizations used these unaffiliated students, maneuvering them into confrontations that they would not otherwise have undertaken. But it is also true that the legitimate issues raised by such organizations often spurred sincere, spontaneous action by students who shared the political interests of New Left activists but had previously remained uncommitted because of apathy or preoccupation with other matters.

The best-known organization of the New Left, and the one that has been most deeply involved in the politics of confrontation, is Students for a Democratic Society. SDS was formed in 1960 as an outgrowth of an earlier organization known as the Student League for Industrial Democracy (SLID). The constitution of SDS describes the organization as "an association of young people on the left." "Liberals and radicals, activists and scholars, students and faculty" were invited to join. In 1962, at a meeting in Port Huron, Michigan, SDS drew up a statement of immediate programs and policies that came to be known as the Port Huron Statement:

> We are people of this generation, bred in at least modern comfort, housed in universities, looking uncomfortably to the world we inherit. Our work is guided by the sense that we may be the last generation in the experiment with living. . . . We ourselves are imbued with urgency, yet the message of our society is that there is no viable alternative to the present. . . .
>
> Feeling the press of complexity upon the emptiness of life, people are fearful of the thought that at any moment things might thrust out of control. They fear change itself, since change might smash whatever invisible frame holds back chaos for them now. For most Americans, all crusades are suspect, threatening. . . .
>
> If student movements for change are rarities still on the

campus scene, what is commonplace there? The real campus, the familiar campus, is a place of private people, engaged in their notorious "inner emigration." It is a place of commitment to business as usual, getting ahead, playing it cool. It is a place of mass affirmation of the Twist, but mass reluctance toward the controversial public stance. Rules are accepted as "inevitable," bureaucracy as "just circumstances," irrelevance as "scholarship," selflessness as "martyrdom."

SDS set out to change all that. And, with the help of other organizations and many unaffiliated students, it has made remarkable strides. While not all campuses or even most are hotbeds of radicalism, political activism on the campus has certainly increased enormously since the Port Huron days of 1962. Today, there are SDS chapters on hundreds of American campuses. And the organization is currently involved in a nationwide campaign to organize chapters in high schools, community colleges, and trade schools.

Among the most highly publicized confrontations staged by SDS—one that gained the organization many supporters and many opponents—was a student uprising at Columbia University in New York City. The chief issue was Columbia's plan to construct a gymnasium in Morningside Park, a recreation area long used by residents of the neighborhood surrounding the university. Many of the residents are poor blacks and Puerto Ricans. SDS and its supporters argued that Columbia had been constantly expanding its campus deeper into the neighborhood, thus driving out poor families. They felt that construction of the university's gym on the park site, depriving the local residents of recreation space, would be the final indignity in Columbia's long history of indifference to the plight of its neighbors.

The SDS branch at Columbia, headed by a student

named Mark Rudd—who eventually became a nationally known figure—mobilized massive demonstrations against the park takeover. Students called strikes, seized university buildings, tried to prevent their nonparticipating colleagues from attending classes, in some cases destroyed property, stole or copied confidential papers in administrators' offices, and otherwise created chaos on campus. Police were called in and made mass arrests with what some students claimed was an excessive use of force. The university was shut down, many students were suspended, and some were denied degrees they had been scheduled to receive.

The massive nature of the demonstrations, the completeness with which they closed down the university, the purported excesses committed by the students, and the controversy over the police tactics all contributed to bringing the Columbia confrontations more attention than most campus uprisings. The confrontations did halt construction of the gymnasium and led to changes among top Columbia administrators. But some critics charged that the extremes of student behavior damaged the cause of campus rebellion to an extent that outweighed whatever benefits might have arisen from the uprising. Certainly, it would be hard to explain how the students' goals could be advanced by, for example, the destruction of university property and the theft of confidential files.

Of course, the campus confrontations that created the greatest commotion—such as those at Columbia—received the most attention from the news media. Thus, the public may have been given a distorted picture of the character of dissent on many college campuses. There is considerable evidence that, for every campus confrontation that led critics to charge students with irresponsibility, there were many more in which the students made their views known responsibly. One report on campus unrest that placed the situation in perspective was prepared for the Carnegie Commission on Higher Education by Richard E. Peterson, a research psychologist, and John A. Bilorusky of the University of Cincinnati. They interviewed all college presidents in the country and found that on only about 100 of the nation's 2,500 campuses had the presidents felt that protests had escalated into "excesses, violence and near-paralysis of the institutions." At many more colleges, the report said, "the response was peaceful, resourceful and but briefly disruptive." And, the report continued, on 1,100 campuses the turmoil sweeping through other colleges and universities "made no appreciable impact at all."

Still, there were some respected observers of the campus scene who felt students' employment of confrontation tactics had gotten out of hand. Among the critics was John R. Searle, a philosophy professor at Berkeley. At one time Searle had been a faculty leader of Berkeley's Free Speech Movement. Later he had been special assistant to the Chancellor for Student Affairs. His experience led him to write a magazine article entitled "A Foolproof Scenario for Student Revolts." Although written at least partly with tongue in cheek, the article seemed to summarize accurately the abuses of confrontation strategy in some campus protests.

Searle said the majority of such protests could be broken down into three stages. In Stage One, his mock advice suggested, students should pick any issue on which the university administration cannot give in—an issue related to what he called a Sacred Topic, such as First Amendment rights, race, or the war in Southeast Asia. Then, knowing that the university will reject it, the students must make their demand to the administration. "The demand has to be presented in the maximally confrontationalist style," Searle wrote. "This usually requires a demonstration of some sort, and sit-ins are not uncommon at this stage, though a 'mass meeting' or march to present your demands will often do as well."

In Stage Two, he advised, the strategy is to make university authorities the target of the protest. For example, if university officials oppose an antiwar sit-in, it should be argued that they must favor war. This strategy, Searle said, will increase the number of demonstrators, make the protest leaders television celebrities, and "dignify the uproar."

In Stage Three, the proposed strategy is to force the administration to call in the police. There will be widespread revulsion to the use of armed force on the campus, Searle wrote. Sympathetic professors will become active in the protest, and opposition to the student movement will collapse. The original issue will be forgotten, but the college president will probably be fired, the faculty set to bickering, and the campus closed. "The forces of 'progress' will have triumphed," he concluded.

A more somber critique of campus confrontations was offered in a study by Lewis Feuer, a professor of sociology at the University of Toronto who formerly taught at Berkeley. After reviewing the current student protests and those dating back to the nineteenth century in the United States and abroad, Feuer concluded that all campus rebellions are "symbolic parricide" (murder of one's parents) in which a young generation tries to humiliate and overthrow the institutions of its parents, regardless of the political issues or consequences. "Student movements are the most sincerely selfless and altruistic the world has seen," Feuer said in an interview. "But they are distorted and pulled toward extreme and amoral means because the driving energy comes from unconscious sources. The pattern is the same in practically every country. The movement is rooted in altruism, a concern for establishing community and overcoming alienation. It begins by celebrating liberal democratic values and usually ends by discrediting those values for the whole society...."

Feuer said that adult leaders of vast political movements, in effect, use students by whipping up fervor among them. Then, in order to avoid leaving the impression that the students are being controlled by their elders, the adults allow young leaders to emerge and carry the movements forward. At some point of crisis, such as the arrival of police on campus, Feuer said the student leaders appeal to "generational solidarity"—that is, they urge their young followers to unite against such older-generation representatives as the police and university administrators. "The struggle is finally revealed in its true aspect," Feuer said. For at that point, he feels, the students' desire to punish the older generation can easily override rational politics and the initial goals of the movements.

"If we can make this irrational element overt, then perhaps student altruism won't flow into self-destructive channels," Feuer commented. "If we don't want it [self-destructive campus confrontation] to happen again and again, it's important to get moderates, liberals and conservatives to assert themselves on campus. If the whole campus can be involved in electing a student government willing to take over disciplinary matters in case of an outbreak, a rational position may be worked out."

At this stage, it is too early to say whether such judgments as Feuer's will be borne out by history. Certainly, student activists have committed unnecessary violence on some campuses. But whether campus confrontations on the whole will be proved "self-destructive" is something else. It is clear, even at this early juncture, that the confrontation politics practiced by students has produced numerous beneficial results. On many campuses, ombudsmen (university officials who investigate complaints) now serve as buffers between the students and the faculty and administration. Legitimate student grievances are being sympathetically received with increasing frequency. In addition, students are being delegated larger roles in determining how their schools should be operated.

At the University of Wisconsin, for instance, students have been given voting seats on several faculty policy-making committees. The president of the student government has been given a voting seat on the City-University Coordinating Committee. And students have been given advisory roles in groups deciding on faculty qualifications and courses. The university's assistant dean of students, Elmer E. Meyer, Jr., attributes the increasing authority given Wisconsin students directly to the confrontation movement. The movement, he says, "certainly speeded up the process" by which faculty members became more willing to include students on policy-making bodies.

At Cornell, the movement generally is credited with bringing about an investigation of the "quality of undergraduate education," resulting in the formation of a group known as "Students for Education." At Northwestern University, a series of seminars previously attended only by faculty members was opened to students. At the University of Oregon, students were given a voice in faculty promotions and granting of tenure. At Stanford University, a "committee of fifteen"—composed of five students, five teachers, and five administrators—was established to recommend policy changes. At Colorado State College, administrators put into effect a "student bill of rights." And comparable reforms were made at hundreds of other colleges and universities. Some may argue that such reforms would have come in time without the use of confrontation tactics, but there is no doubt that the confrontation strategy speeded the process and in some cases produced beneficial changes that would never have been achieved through more traditional forms of student action.

The next two chapters will examine the most tragic campus confrontation in recent years, the reactions to it, and the resulting recommendations for making both schools and American society as a whole more responsive to the demands of young citizens.

7
Tragedy at Kent State

IT HAS been said, with some justification, that the tragic confrontation that left four students dead at Kent State University in Ohio could have occurred on virtually any campus in the country. For that reason, it is important to understand just what happened at Kent State if such catastrophies are to be prevented in the future. Much has been said and written, in passion and sorrow, about the events of Kent State. But relatively few attempts have been made to examine the confrontation dispassionately with an eye toward learning something constructive, rather than merely assessing blame.

What follows is such an attempt. It seeks to place the Kent State tragedy in its proper perspective in the history of confrontation politics. Its aim is not to designate heroes or villains but rather to study the possible consequences of confrontations in which sudden, unexpected events convert seemingly minor acts of violence into major holocausts.

There is a widely held belief that the Kent State confrontation was a spontaneous student reaction to President Richard M. Nixon's decision to send American troops into

Cambodia in May 1970. But the truth of the matter is not nearly that simple. Trouble had been brewing for some time at Kent State, and the Cambodian issue was merely the spark that ignited the dry tinder of discontent.

Kent State is a complex of ninety-seven buildings accommodating about twenty-one thousand students. Its campus, set on a series of rolling hills, is eleven miles from Akron. Eighty-five percent of its students are from Ohio, and until the 1970 confrontation they were generally considered conservative politically. Before 1968, the year President Nixon was elected, the biggest commotion in Kent State's history had been caused by a mass panty raid ten years earlier.

But in 1968 the first signs of confrontation politics began to appear on the campus. That fall members of the Oakland, California, police department—then involved in a violent struggle with the Black Panther Party—made a trip to Kent State to try to recruit potential police trainees. In protest of the recruitment drive, about 150 members of the Kent State chapter of Students for a Democratic Society and about 100 members of an organization named the Black United Students (BUS) conducted a sit-in at the university's student-activities center. The administration ordered pictures taken of all the demonstrators, and threatened to have them arrested. In response, about 300 black students—half the blacks on the campus—boycotted classes for three days. They returned only when University President Robert White announced there was insufficient evidence to sustain criminal charges against those who had taken part in the sit-in.

SDS members, considering White's decision a victory for their cause, decided to stage further confrontations. In April 1969 SDS led demonstrations supporting a number of demands, including the abolition of ROTC programs on campus. One demonstration led to a scuffle with campus police. Another resulted in the arrest of fifty-eight students inside Kent State's music and speech building. The administration contended the students had seized the building; the students insisted they had been locked in.

In the aftermath of the demonstrations, the administration banned SDS from the campus. In addition, four SDS leaders were sentenced to six-month jail terms on assault charges stemming from the previous confrontations. Campus radicals and liberals considered the ban on SDS repressive, and felt it forecast future attempts to stifle student dissent. Cautiously but intensely, they began preparing the way for further tests of the strategy of confrontation. Administrators and activists viewed each other warily for a time, like prize fighters circling in the ring, waiting for an opening.

Then, during this period of tension, President Nixon announced on the night of April 30, 1970, his intention to send troops into Cambodia. By 7 o'clock the next morning, the wheels were already in motion for a confrontation at Kent State—one that might well have arisen over some other issue but now would be focused on the Cambodia invasion. A group of students with left-wing leanings met informally to discuss what might be done. Chris Plant, a graduate student in history, suggested forming a new organization to protest the United States' purported racism and exploitation of smaller countries. As a first step, Plant proposed a demonstration at noon that day in which a copy of the United States Constitution would be buried on the Kent State Commons, a wide lawn at the center of the campus.

At noon about five hundred students were gathered on the Commons. Plant made a brief speech in which he called the President "an outlaw." A fellow graduate student, Steve Sharoff, asked in another speech for the abolition of the ROTC program. Sharoff produced a copy of the Constitution torn from the pages of a sixth-grade history book. He dug a hole a few inches deep and buried the document, as Plant told the group, "We inter the Constitution because it has been murdered by the Chief Executive of the United States." University officials kept close watch on the demonstration, but gave no orders for campus police to break it up.

Just before the demonstration ended, someone shouted, "Shall we meet again to plan a real antiwar organization?" Most of the demonstrators shouted back: "Yes!" They agreed to gather at noon the following Monday, May 4. The demonstrators had no way of knowing it at the time, of course, but that Monday would be the day of the climactic and fatal confrontation. As the initial demonstration on May 1 ended peacefully, word was passed through the crowd: "There's going to be street action downtown tonight." No one knew what form this street action might take, but the message left an air of expectation and excitement among the demonstrators.

Three hours after the burying of the Constitution, there was another demonstration on the Commons—this one led by the Black United Students. University President White had been disturbed by a recent editorial in the BUS newspaper, *Black Watch*, which had exhorted its readers: "End all forms of mental mistreatment of black minds. This calls for the firing or, if need be, killing of all racist deans, professors, coaches or university presidents." White had also been deeply concerned over President Nixon's speech, fearing it might touch off troubles on various campuses—including, perhaps, his own. He was due to leave Kent to attend a meeting of educators in Iowa, and now he wondered if it would be wise to be away from the campus during a period of potential turmoil. In an effort to gauge the temper of the students, he observed the BUS demonstration.

The general tenor of the demonstration was so moderate that White decided he could prudently make the trip to Iowa. He boarded a plane at 5:30 that afternoon. The next time he would see his campus, the responsibility for its control would be out of his hands, by order of the Governor of Ohio.

After the peaceful end of the BUS demonstration and the departure of White for Iowa, the next significant events took place that night in the downtown area of the city of Kent. The scene was a section of North Water Street known as "the Strip," where there were a half-dozen taverns frequented not only by Kent State students but also by many young men and women from neighboring cities and campuses. It was a hot night and the interiors of the taverns were stuffy, so many of the students drifted outside to the streets to get some air. Before long, a sizable crowd had formed. Perhaps because of the tension created by the day's two demonstrations, many of the students were jumpier than usual. Besides, some of them knew that street action had been promised for that night. In any event, when someone set off a string of firecrackers, they were mistaken for gunshots. There was a sudden commotion in the crowd. A beer bottle was tossed at a passing car, breaking one of its windows.

Joseph Bujack, owner of a tavern called J.B.'s, did not like the looks of the crowd outside. He knew most of the people who came to the bars on the Strip, but many of those he now saw outside were strangers. One of the strangers was carrying a Vietcong flag; others were shouting antiwar slogans. Bujack went looking for Robert DeFluiter, an off-duty policeman who worked part time as a bouncer for taverns on the Strip.

When he found the officer, Bujack expressed fear about the growing crowd in the streets. DeFluiter agreed that trouble might be brewing, and suggested that Bujack telephone police headquarters to request that a squad car be sent to the scene. Bujack made the call at 10:42 P.M. A short time later a police car pulled into the Strip. It was immediately struck with a beer bottle, but the two officers inside could not catch the person responsible for the incident, and they drove away.

A few minutes later, when an elderly couple drove through the Strip in an old car, some of the students blocked their way and tried to get them to turn back. But the driver refused and edged forward slowly until his car nudged one of the students slightly. A swarm of students crowded around the car, rocking it back and forth and breaking its windows. Amid a torrent of flying beer bottles the driver rammed his way through the crowd and got away with his passenger.

The crowd continued to grow, and it became increasingly unruly. With heightening intensity, the students shouted antiwar slogans—in particular, denunciations of the Cambodia intervention. What appears to have started as a relatively aimless outburst of student rambunctiousness was beginning to take on a clear focus: protest of the President's announcement. It cannot be said for certain whether this development came about by accident or design. The important factor is that it did come about, converting the subsequent events into acts of political confrontation.

Several more police cars cruised through the Strip; they were bombarded with bottles and drove away. Officer DeFluiter heatedly telephoned the police dispatcher and told him, "If you're not going to send men to make arrests, don't send any more cars through here. This crowd is getting real bad." By that time police officials recognized they had a serious situation on their hands. Emergency calls were sent out to off-duty policemen, ordering them to report immediately to police headquarters to cope with a "riot in progress."

Meanwhile, the demonstrators put three cars across the Strip and blocked the street. They then started a bonfire in the middle of the street, and set fire to a small shed nearby. Shortly after midnight, about twenty policemen arrived. They took no overt action to provoke the demonstrators. But apparently their mere presence—in full riot dress—was interpreted by both students and non-students in the crowd as a provocation in itself. Many of the demonstrators began smashing tavern windows.

At 12:30 A.M. on Saturday, May 2, Kent Mayor LeRoy Satrom declared a state of emergency. He then telephoned the office of Ohio Governor James Rhodes and advised one of the Governor's aides that he considered the situation serious. Although he was not requesting National Guard help at the time, Satrom said he might be forced to do so later. A short time afterward the Mayor went to the Strip in a police car. He ordered the bars closed and placed the city under curfew. But rather than helping the situation, the closing of the bars made it worse. Many of the young people had remained in the bars, despite the disturbance on the streets. The closing of the taverns merely forced them outside, swelling the throng that the police had to handle. In addition, many of those ordered out of the bars were angry because they had just bought drinks and had not been allowed to finish them.

Demonstrators continued smashing windows, eventually breaking about fifty of them in downtown business places. A crowd of about five hundred demonstrators then turned its anger on the policemen, showering them with rocks and bottles. Finally, at 1:42 A.M., policemen wearing gas masks fired round after round of tear gas into the crowd. Many of the students seemed bent on further confrontations, but a strange quirk of fate occurred at this point to forestall additional violence. By coincidence, a serious traffic accident took place near the scene of the tear-gas incident. Their attention diverted by the accident, students and police alike abandoned their assaults on each other to lend a hand at the accident scene. By 2 A.M., the first night of trouble at Kent State was over. The students drifted back to their rooms and the police abandoned their positions.

All told, 14 persons—none of them a leader of the disturbance—had been arrested. Property damage, originally estimated at more than $100,000, was later fixed at $10-000. Although the disturbance had been the worst in Kent's history, it seemed mild compared with the sort of violent confrontations Americans had become accustomed to viewing on television newscasts. Still, for the citizens of Kent the events were alarming. This was not Berkeley or Columbia. This was Kent, in the heartland of what has come to be known as "middle America." Was the Friday night riot a single aberration or did it forecast days and weeks of turmoil? Nobody could say, but local citizens and officials, conditioned by news coverage of similar disturbances elsewhere, feared the worst. Their fears were compounded by what they saw and heard when they awoke Saturday morning.

One Kent businessman, Ervin Hoefler, who operated a music shop, said a young, bearded man entered his store Saturday and told him, "I'd advise you to put an antiwar sign up in your window or you might get burned out tonight." Mayor Satrom received reports that some Kent State students were keeping weapons on the campus and that members of the Weathermen—the most militant faction of SDS—had been seen in the crowd involved in the Friday night riot. Later investigation of these reports revealed little evidence to support them. But it seems clear that the Mayor sincerely believed them at the time; as a result, he may have overreacted. The reports plus the Friday night disturbance and several threats of the kind received by merchant Hoefler persuaded Satrom that local law enforcement might be incapable of maintaining order in case of further trouble. Thus, at 5:27 Saturday afternoon, he asked state officials to send National Guardsmen into Kent. Governor Rhodes complied, and the Guardsmen started rolling into town shortly after 7 P.M.

Satrom also ordered an 8 P.M. curfew, confining Kent State students to the campus on Saturday night. The decisions to call in the Guard and order the curfew have been severely criticized in the light of ensuing events. Among the critics of the curfew was Kent State senior, Jeff Sallot, who argued that the decision to keep the students on campus was part of a self-fulfilling prophecy that new violence would develop. "If it hadn't been for the curfew, I think everyone would have gone his own way," Sallot said. "As it was, everyone started crowding up on campus."

In the crowd that formed, the prevailing sentiment favored demonstrating opposition to the Cambodian intervention by mounting some sort of confrontation centered on the Kent State ROTC building. The building was a rickety old barracks that served as headquarters for the 173 student cadets who voluntarily participated in the ROTC program. Nobody lived in the building; it was used merely for storage and training purposes. Despite its unimposing appearance, it was the closest thing Kent State possessed to a symbol of military authority—the authority involved in the Vietnam war and the Cambodian intervention.

When the students decided to make the building their rallying point, they passed word to others still in the dormitories to come down and join them. By 8:10 P.M. the crowd had grown to about two thousand. Some students began throwing rocks through the barracks windows. Others tried to set the building on fire, but failed.

Then, shortly before 8:30, a young man soaked a rag in the gasoline tank of a parked motorcycle, ran up to a broken window, ignited the rag, and held it against a curtain until the fire took hold. At about the same time, two other demonstrators ran to a window with two railroad flares, ignited them, and tossed them through the window. These fires quickly ate up curtains and walls while the demonstrators chanted: "Burn, baby, burn!" As the fire swept through other sections of the wooden building, someone called the fire department.

When a fire truck arrived, students prevented the firemen from fighting the blaze. By that time smoke was billowing from the building. Finally, a force of eighteen campus policemen, who had been waiting for orders to intervene, rushed to the scene in gas masks and helmets. "Pigs! Pigs!" the demonstrators yelled. Students bombarded the officers with rocks and firecrackers. The diversion of the demonstrators' attention allowed the firemen to try to put out the blaze. They almost got the fire under control, but then left it smoldering as the students showered them with rocks.

Although the campus police fired tear gas to drive the students back, they were unable to establish clear control of the area. Ultimately, National Guardsmen arrived and helped establish order. By that time, however, the ROTC building had burned down to a pile of rubble—with a loss estimated at $50,000 for the structure and another $35,000 for the equipment inside. It was midnight before the campus was cleared of demonstrators.

The next morning, Governor Rhodes flew to Kent and met with Mayor Satrom, a National Guard General, the head of the state highway patrol, and the local district attorney. They sat around a table in a firehouse and discussed what should be done. Also in the room, but not seated at the table or invited to take active roles in the discussion, were three vice-presidents and two other officials of the university.

Governor Rhodes made the position of the university administrators plain at the outset of the meeting. He pointed a fimger at them and remarked: "You university people stay out of this. We're taking over now." Since Kent State was a state university, subject to the Governor's authority, the administrators had no choice but to comply.

Several times Rhodes said to those present, "We have got to keep this university open at all costs. To close it down would be to play into the hands of all the dissident elements that are trying to do just that." During the meeting an aide interrupted the Governor to say that a crowd of newsmen was outside, demanding a press conference. At this point, in the view of some observers, political considerations influenced Rhodes's behavior. Rhodes was then involved in a bitter primary fight with Robert Taft for the Republican nomination for a U.S. Senate seat. With the primary only two days away, Taft was thought to be leading (he eventually won both the primary and the general election). According to some critics, Rhodes believed that he could use the Kent disruptions to improve his image, by talking and acting tough with the student demonstrators. In the meeting with the officials the Governor had appeared firm but not provocative. When he went out to meet the press, however, his attitude seemed to border on belligerence.

"We've seen here in the city of Kent probably the most vicious form of campus-oriented violence yet perpetrated by dissident groups in the state of Ohio," Rhodes told the newsmen. "We're going to employ every force of law that we have under our authority. . . . The same group [of agitators] that we're dealing with here today—and there are three or four of them [in the group]—they only have one thing in mind and that is to destroy higher education in Ohio. You cannot continue to set fires to buildings that are worth five and ten million dollars. . . . No one is safe here. . . .

"These people just move from one campus to another and terrorize a community. They're worse than the Brown Shirts and the communist element and also the night-riders in the vigilantes. They're the worst type of people that we harbor in America. I think that we are up against the strongest, [most] well-trained militant group that has ever assembled in America. We are going to eradicate the problems; we're not going to treat the symptoms. There is no sanctuary for these people to burn buildings down. . . . It's over with in Ohio. . . ."

No matter what his motivation, it is clear that Rhodes's statements to the press contained several inaccuracies, and even more contentions that were subject to serious challenge. For example, his statement that the events in Kent constituted "the most vicious form of campus-oriented violence yet perpetrated" in Ohio was a gross exaggeration. The violence in Kent to that point had been far less serious than previous campus disorders in Columbus, Athens, and Oxford, Ohio. The Governor's claim that the Kent demonstrators had set fire to buildings "worth five and ten million dollars" was also inaccurate: the ROTC building had been worth $50,000 and its equipment an additional $35,000. Similarly, Rhodes's contention that the Kent protesters constituted "the strongest, [most] well-trained militant group that has ever assembled in America" seemed patently false, although it was accepted as gospel by many citizens of Ohio and other states.

Perhaps more important than these inaccuracies was the

governor's use of such inflammatory phrases as "worse than the Brown Shirts and the communist element" in referring to the demonstrators. "Brown Shirts," an allusion to the Nazis, particularly enraged some students. In a previous statement President Nixon had referred generally to student demonstrators as "bums." On the Kent State campus, one girl who had not yet participated in any violence asked, "If the President thinks I'm a bum and the Governor thinks I'm a Nazi, what does it matter how I act?"

Her reaction was echoed by many other Kent State students. And Rhodes's words had a significant effect on others in Kent as well. Myron J. Lunine, dean of the Honors College and professor of political science at Kent State, said the Governor's statements substantially increased the National Guardsmen's animosity toward the demonstrators. "In addition, the head of one of the state's police organizations had warned the Guardsmen to beware of snipers, who could be expected to go into action soon," Lunine said. "What conclusions could the Guardsmen reach but that the students were an evil lot against whom they would have to defend themselves, perhaps with bullets? Words were very important that weekend, and always in a destructive direction."

When Governor Rhodes finished his visit to Kent on Sunday, he met briefly with returning Kent State President White at the local airport. He told White the campus was being besieged by "outside agitators" and instructed the educator to try to keep the university open. The claim of "outside agitators" is made frequently against those who engage in confrontation politics. In some cases it is based on fact. In the case of Kent State no solid evidence has been found to support the contention, as with many other claims made by Rhodes. Rhodes left after talking with White, and neither returned to Kent, nor offered further advice to those on the scene. Rhodes had a strenuous schedule to maintain in his race for the Senate nomination.

In his wake he left a city and a campus that were in perhaps greater turmoil than before his visit. His strong words had not sat well with most students. They had further solidified the barrier between the campus community and the townspeople, local officials, and Guardsmen. Moreover, the Governor's insistence on keeping the campus open at all costs virtually guaranteed further trouble.

The new trouble began Sunday night at a campus gate. About two hundred students sat down in a street just off the campus, while another five hundred sat behind them on university property. They said they were demonstrating for removal of the National Guardsmen, lifting of the Mayor's curfew, and amnesty for students arrested during previous protests. The demonstration started in an orderly fashion.

Police and National Guardsmen had arrived by 11 P.M. The students told them they wanted to meet with President White or Mayor Satrom to discuss their demands. Some students later claimed they had been promised that the university president or the Mayor would soon be there. Actually, the Mayor had been notified of the students' request and was on his way to the scene, but White knew nothing about the request. Before the Mayor's arrival, however, a National Guard colonel told the students they were violating the curfew. He then read them the state's riot law, which permits jail terms up to three years for violators. Although there had been no disorder or anything resembling a riot at that point—simply a purported violation of the curfew—the colonel warned the demonstrators that their actions constituted breaking the riot law. He then ordered his men to disperse the crowd.

The Guardsmen fired tear gas. The students scattered,

but began pelting the Guardsmen with rocks. Many of the students shouted that they had been betrayed—that they had been promised the Mayor or the university's President would discuss their demands, but that instead the tear gas had been fired. The first student injuries of the weekend occurred during the dispersal of the crowd when two students were pricked by Guardsmen's bayonets, but the Sunday night disturbance did not escalate into a major battle. Students eventually returned to their rooms without causing serious injuries or property damage. But the tension continued to build, and the next day it would explode.

At two minutes before noon on Monday, May 4, someone began ringing an old railroad-engine bell that had been brought to Kent State twenty years earlier and installed as the official Victory Bell. Whenever the university won an important sports event, the bell was rung. It was also rung for another purpose: to summon students to meet on the Commons just below an area of the campus known as Blanket Hill. This day, there was no victory to celebrate; the ringing of the bell was clearly a summons.

Students converged on the Commons, and, almost at the same time, National Guardsmen arrived to disperse them. A campus police car and a National Guard jeep, each equipped with a bullhorn, circled the students. From the bullhorns came identical messages: "This assembly is unlawful. The crowd must disperse at this time. This is an order."

But the crowd was in no mood to disperse. Students felt it was their campus and they had a right to congregate on it. This was a peaceful assembly, they contended, and the Constitution guaranteed them the right of free assembly. Besides, it had been known ever since the previous Friday, when the copy of the Constitution had been buried, that another meeting had been called for noon Monday. Why, the students asked, were they being told at this late hour that they couldn't meet? (Actually, beginning at 11:15 A.M. the campus radio station—at the request of the National Guard—had been broadcasting a warning that all outdoor gatherings had been banned by order of the Governor, and that violators might be arrested. But most students never heard the warning, either because they were attending classes at the time or because they were not tuned to the broadcasts. Moreover, a number of professors, unaware of the ban, had dismissed classes early, specifically instructing the students to attend the noon rally.)

When the students on the Commons heard the orders to disperse, they began hooting and shouting slogans. "Off the pigs! Off the pigs!" some of them yelled. "Two-four-six-eight, we don't want your fascist state! One-two-three-four, we don't want your———war!"

Again, the bullhorns commanded: "Disperse!" A rock flew through the air and hit the National Guard jeep. Word was passed to the Guardsmen: "If you have not already done so, load and lock [your weapons]. Prepare for gas attack." Next, National Guard General Robert H. Canterbury ordered: "Prepare to move out and disperse this mob."

Although there were about 800 Guardsmen at Kent, the contingent involved in this operation appears to have numbered only 113. The size of the crowd of demonstrators and bystanders has been variously estimated at from 800 to 1,500. General Canterbury's dispersal plan called for the Guardsmen to force the demonstrators back from the Commons in a southwesterly direction, toward Blanket Hill. The Guardsmen would then push the students down the far side of Blanket Hill toward a football practice field and there make them scatter.

Before Canterbury could put this plan into operation, an unidentified spokesman for the students ran up to him and said, "General, you must not march against the students." Canterbury replied that the students were congregating illegally. "These students are going to have to find out what law and order is all about," he said. The general then ordered his men to fire tear-gas canisters into the crowd.

Some of the students ran forward, grabbed the canisters, and tossed them back at the Guardsmen. Others picked up rocks and threw them at the troops. The Guardsmen continued firing tear gas as they pursued the demonstrators. There were a few hand-to-hand altercations between Guardsmen and students. But gradually the demonstrators did retreat up Blanket Hill, and some of them fled down the other side of the slope. As they ran, they threw heavy chunks of concrete block and pieces of wood studded with nails at the troops, and kept up a steady verbal barrage. Some students cursed the troops viciously. Others taunted them with epithets such as "fascists" and "toy soldiers."

At this point, the Guardsmen made what must be considered in retrospect a tactical mistake: they forced the retreating students toward the practice field. But they apparently failed to recognize that if they carried their plan to its logical conclusion, they would find themselves surrounded on several sides by the demonstrators and on the remaining sides by tall chain-link fences topped with barbed wire. Thus, in order to escape from their predicament, they would have to go back in the same direction from which they had come—giving the students the impression they were retreating.

When the students realized the Guardsmen were pinned with their backs to the chain-link fences, they began to charge toward the troops, throwing rocks and tear-gas canisters picked up from the ground. At that point not enough students were involved in the charges to surround the Guardsmen. There were wide spaces through which the Guardsmen could have retreated, but they chose to stand their ground. Suddenly sixteen men belonging to a Guard contingent known as G Troop, who thought their tear-gas supply had run out, crouched in firing positions and aimed their M-1 rifles at some of the students.

Had the Guardsmen fired at that point, the result could have been wholesale slaughter. But they did not. Nobody gave a command to fire, and the Guardsmen discovered that they were not out of tear gas after all. About this time, orders were given for the Guardsmen to regroup and move back toward the burned-out ROTC building. Those who had knelt in firing position rose and began to regroup.

The Guardsmen were stifling inside their gas masks. They had been humiliated by the incident at the chain-link fences, and realized that they looked foolish now as they retreated from the ground they had taken. As the Guardsmen climbed back up Blanket Hill, some students followed and taunted them. But the troops certainly didn't appear in any imminent danger. They had a clear route back to the ROTC building. The only large gathering of students was on the Guardsmen's right flank, a good seventy yards away.

Suddenly, however, some of the Guardsmen closest to that group of students stopped, turned around, and, for reasons that have never been fully explained, placed their rifles in the "ready" position. A gunshot rang out. Then, after a pause of perhaps two seconds, there was a barrage of shots. After another brief pause, there was a fresh burst, then another pause, then two last shots. The gunfire (which was tape-recorded by three Kent State journalism students) lasted thirteen seconds. From all available evidence, fifty-five bullets from M-1 rifles, five pistol shots, and one shotgun blast were fired. No credible evidence has shown that anyone except Guardsmen did any firing. Twenty-eight of the Guardsmen apparently fired their weapons, but some obviously aimed into the air or above the heads of the demonstrators. Others just as obviously fired directly into the crowd.

When the shooting ended, four students lay dead and nine others were sprawled on the grass with relatively serious bullet wounds. Of the Guardsmen's victims, eleven were men and two were women. What were these students doing at the time of the shooting, and how much of a threat, if any, did they pose to the Guardsmen? Some of the answers are apparent, some not. Of those who were shot, the closest victim was 71 feet away from the Guardsmen and the farthest 745 feet away. Of the four who were killed, the closest was 265 feet away and the farthest 390 feet away. It seems obvious that, no matter what threat the entire mass of students posed to the Guardsmen, the students who were shot, and particularly those who were killed, presented little or no immediate threat. Considering the weapons available to them, they were too far away to be much of a menace.

The dead students were Allison Krause, a nineteen-year-old freshman from Pittsburgh, Pennsylvania; Sandra Scheuer, a twenty-year-old junior from Youngstown, Ohio; Jeffrey Miller, a twenty-year-old transfer student from Michigan State whose home was in Plainview, New York; and William Schroeder, a nineteen-year-old sophomore from Lorain, Ohio.

Miss Krause, an honor student, believed in protest but not in violence. She had marched in peace demonstrations, but her attitude was perhaps best summed up by an incident that occurred the day before her death: She had walked up to a Guardsman, smiled, placed a flower in his gun barrel, and told him, "Flowers are better than bullets." All accounts indicate that during the disturbance on the day of her death, she was merely a spectator who got caught in the line of fire.

Miss Scheuer, also an honor student, was not even a spectator, and had taken no part in previous demonstrations. At the time of the Friday night disturbance she was roller skating. When the ROTC building was burned she was studying for an examination. At the time of the Sunday night sit-in she was sitting in the living room of the off-campus house in which she lived. And at the time of the disturbance that took her life she was walking from a speech-therapy class and trying to get out of the way of the turmoil when a bullet struck her in the neck and killed her.

Miller had not been downtown during the Friday night disturbance, had watched but not participated in the burning of the ROTC building, and had taken part in the sit-in Sunday night. All evidence indicates that he had taken no part in the violence on Monday, but simply had been watching the action when he was fatally shot.

Schroeder was the prototype of the all-American boy: a former Eagle Scout, a high school basketball and track star with excellent grades. Far from wanting the ROTC building burned down, he had been angered by the arson. He was attending Kent State on an ROTC scholarship that paid his full tuition and fees plus $50 a month. In fact, he was the second-ranking student in the ROTC unit. All available evidence indicates he took no part in any of the confrontations, and was merely a spectator at the disturbance in which he was killed.

Thus, four students who apparently had taken no action against the Guardsmen had been slain by them. Was there any justification for the resort to gunfire? What did this tragic incident teach about the uses of confrontation politics? What were the results of the Kent State protest? And what were the national ramifications?

These questions and others will be addressed in the next chapter.

8

The Aftermath of Violence

THE combination of President Nixon's Cambodia decision and the Kent State catastrophe hurled much of the nation into the arena of confrontation politics. More than one hundred thousand protesters demanding an American pullout from Southeast Asia descended on Washington, D.C., for demonstrations that were basically peaceful. Confrontations were staged on hundreds of campuses in every section of the country, from Bowdoin College in Maine to the University of Miami, from Harvard to Berkeley.

In Mississippi another tragic outbreak of violence occurred when students clashed with law-enforcement officers on the campus of the predominantly black Jackson State College. As students bombarded them with rocks and bottles, the officers opened fire with shotguns and other firearms. Two students, Phillip L. Gibbs and James Earl Green, were killed, and twelve others were wounded.

At California's Whittier College, where President Nixon had earned his bachelor's degree, 30 percent of the student body angrily protested his policies. At the Duke University Law School, where the President had earned his law degree, his portrait was removed from the wall of a moot courtroom and placed in storage. At Manhattan's Finch College, the alma mater of Nixon's daughter Tricia, the students went on strike. At the University of Nebraska, in the center of an area that had long been considered "Nixon country," students seized the ROTC headquarters. At the University of Arizona students staged the first demonstration in the history of the campus.

At the University of Wisconsin, eighty-three students were arrested after twenty major fire bombings. At the University of New Mexico dissenting students fought with their "straight" colleagues over whether a flag should be lowered to half-staff to honor the Kent State dead; three of the dissenters came away from the battle with knife wounds.

In many cases protests were supported by college officials. At Oberlin College, for example, President Robert Carr canceled final exams, gave all students credit for their courses, and officially turned the campus over to activists planning antiwar demonstrations.

A case can be made that the Kent State confrontation, calamitous as it was, served several useful purposes, at least in the eyes of antiwar advocates. It galvanized public opinion against the war and revitalized what had been a fading antiwar movement. Moreover, some contend that the tragedy and its aftermath persuaded the Nixon administration to pull American troops out of Cambodia far sooner than had been planned originally. The President, who had said earlier he would not allow himself to be swayed by protesters, unexpectedly appeared in the midst of the Washington demonstrators at one point to try to explain his position on the Cambodian intervention. "I know you think we are a bunch of so-and-sos," Nixon told the young activists. "I know you want to get the war over. Sure, you came here to demonstrate and shout your slogans. That's all right. Just keep it peaceful. Have a good time in Washington, and don't go away bitter." But many of the demonstrators did go away bitter, convinced that the government was not responsive to their demands. Whether their protests ultimately did influence the President to pull out of Cambodia earlier than scheduled must be left for future historians to decide. In the meantime it can be said that the mass outpouring of anti-government sentiment that followed the Kent State affair was one of the largest in recent history.

While the protests continued, several investigations were launched to try to discover precisely what had happened at Kent State, why it had happened, and, even more important, what the causes and consequences of national campus unrest were. The investigations sometimes produced conflicting findings.

The most exhaustive investigation of the events at Kent State was conducted by the FBI on instructions from the Justice Department. The FBI report, which was 7,500 pages, has not been made public. But summaries drawn up by Justice Department lawyers of the evidence gathered by the FBI were leaked to newsmen and elected officials. Among the chief points made in the summaries were:

1. The shooting of the students was unnecessary, since the Guardsmen did not have to resort to gunfire to protect themselves.

2. No Guardsmen were hurt by thrown rocks or other such missiles. No Guardsman was in danger of his life at the time of the shooting.

3. Of the thirteen students struck by bullets, all but four were hit in the back or side—an indication that most of them, at least, posed no threat to the Guardsmen's safety.

4. One Guardsman fired at a student who was merely making an obscene gesture; another fired at a student who was preparing to throw a rock.

5. Most of the Guardsmen who fired did not specifically claim they did so because their lives were in danger. Instead, they generally said that they fired after they heard others fire, or because, after the shooting began, they assumed they had been ordered to fire. (It has never been officially disclosed whether such an order was given.)

6. Six Guardsmen, including two sergeants and a captain, said pointedly that Guardsmen's lives were not in danger and that "it was not a shooting situation." (Some Guard officials claimed their men fired because they sincerely believed their lives were endangered. But the Justice Department summaries said: "We have some reason to believe that the claim by the Guard that their lives were endangered by the students was fabricated subsequent to the event.")

7. Contrary to some claims, there was no sniper firing at the Guardsmen.

8. At least six Guardsmen, identified in the FBI report, were considered by some Justice Department lawyers to be potential defendants in criminal cases arising from the shootings.

For more than a year Attorney General John Mitchell took no formal action on the FBI report. It had been expected that a federal grand jury would be assigned to investigate the facts uncovered by the FBI. But on August 13, 1971, Mitchell announced that no such grand jury would be empaneled. He said a Justice Department review of the events had persuaded him that "there is no credible evidence of a conspiracy between National Guardsmen to shoot students on the campus and that there is no likelihood of successful prosecutions of individual Guardsmen."

Meanwhile, in Kent, a special Ohio grand jury had conducted its own investigation. Contrary to the findings of the FBI and Justice Department officials, this grand jury reported that the Guardsmen fired their weapons "in the sincere and honest belief and under circumstances which would have logically caused them to believe that they would suffer serious bodily injury had they not done so." As a result, the panel ruled, the Guardsmen were "not subject to criminal prosecution."

At the same time, the grand jury did indict twenty-five persons—mostly Kent State students—on charges resulting from the confrontations leading up to the gunplay. In a lengthy report, the panel claimed that "major responsibility" for the Kent State violence "rests clearly with those persons who are charged with the administration of the university." The report accused the university administrators of fostering "an attitude of laxity, over-indulgence and permissiveness," faulted some faculty members for placing an "over-emphasis on the right to dissent," and criticized students for their behavior and purportedly obscene language.

When the criminal cases resulting from the grand jury indictments were called for trial late in 1971, however, only three of the twenty-five defendants were found guilty on any of the charges. Two others were found not guilty, and the cases against the remaining twenty were dismissed by the prosecutor because of what he described as lack of evidence. The supposed lack of evidence in so many cases led critics to question sharply the validity of the grand jury's investigation. If there was insufficient evidence to bring twenty of the twenty-five cases to trial, they asked, why did the grand jury indict the defendants in the first place?

The most significant investigation was conducted by a national commission appointed by President Nixon to look into the broad question of upheaval in the nation's colleges and universities. The commission, headed by former Pennsylvania Governor William Scranton, was called the President's Commission on Campus Unrest. The Commission did specifically investigate the Kent State tragedy. It reported that the firing of weapons by National Guardsmen was "unjustified and inexcusable." It also criticized the actions of some students as "violent, reckless, and irresponsible." Its more important findings, however, were in the broader field of general campus unrest and confrontation. After hearing testimony from numerous students, educators, public officials, law-enforcement officers, and others, the Commission unanimously appealed to President Nixon to lead Americans back from the brink of what it described as a chasm in society so dangerous that it threatened the survival of the nation.

In a call to the American people for unity, the Commission warned:

> The crisis on American campuses has no parallel in the history of the nation. This crisis has roots in divisions of American society as deep as any since the Civil War. The divisions are reflected in violent acts and harsh rhetoric and in the enmity of those Americans who see themselves as occupying opposing camps. Campus unrest reflects and increases a more profound crisis in the nation as a whole. This crisis has two components: a crisis of violence and a crisis of understanding. We fear new violence and growing enmity.

In summarizing its findings on campus unrest, the Commission made the following observations:

> Most student protesters are neither violent nor extremist. But a small minority of politically extreme students and faculty members and a small group of dedicated agitators are bent on destruction of universities through violence in order to gain their own political ends. Perpetrators of violence must be identified, removed from the universities as swiftly as possible and prosecuted vigorously by the appropriate agencies of law enforcement. . . .

Too many students have acted irresponsibly and even dangerously in pursuing their stated goals and expressing their dissent. Too many law-enforcement officers have responded with unwarranted harshness and force in seeking to control disorder. Actions—inactions—of government at all levels have contributed to campus unrest. The words of some political leaders have helped to inflame it. Law-enforcement officers have too often reacted ineptly or overreacted. At times, their response has degenerated into uncontrolled violence.

The nation has been slow to resolve the issues of war and race, which exacerbate divisions within American society and which have contributed to the escalation of student protest and disorder. . . . We must establish respect for the processes of law and tolerance for the exercise of dissent on our campuses and in the nation. . . ."

Among the general recommendations made by the commission were establishment by the government of alternatives to ROTC programs; rejection of demands that entire universities be punished "because of the ideas or excesses of some members"; passage of new laws to control sale, transfer, and possession of explosives and other materials used in arson attempts; greater recruitment by colleges of students and faculty members from minority groups; and a review of federal policies affecting students and universities "to assure that neither the policies nor administration of them threatens the independence or quality of American higher education."

In its more specific recommendations the Commission advised President Nixon:

> We urge that the President exercise his reconciling moral leadership as the first step to prevent violence and create understanding. . . . In the current [1970] political campaign and throughout the years ahead, the President should insist

that no one play irresponsible politics with the issue of "campus unrest."

We recommend that the President take the lead in explaining to the American people the underlying causes of campus unrest and the urgency of our present situation. . . .

To this end, nothing is more important than an end to the war in Indochina. Disaffected students see the war as a symbol of moral crisis in the nation which, in their eyes, deprives even law of its legitimacy. Their dramatic reaction to the Cambodian invasion was a measure of the intensity of their moral recoil.

We urge the President to renew the national commitment to full social justice and to be aware of increasing charges of repression. . . . We recommend that the President take steps to assure that he is continuously informed of the views of students and blacks, important constituencies in this nation.

In its recommendations to students, the Commission said:

Students must accept the responsibility of presenting their ideas in a reasonable and persuasive manner. . . . Students must face the fact that giving moral support to those who are planning violent action is morally despicable. Students should be reminded that language that offends will seldom persuade. Their words have sometimes been as offensive to many Americans as the words of some public officials have been to them. Students should not expect their own views, even if held with great moral intensity, automatically and immediately to determine national policy. . . .

To the nation's colleges and universities, the Commission recommended:

Every university must improve its capability for responding effectively to disorder. Students, faculty and trustees must support these efforts. . . . The university should be an open forum where speakers of every view can be heard. . . .

The university should promulgate a code making clear the limits of permissible conduct and announce in advance what measures it is willing to employ in response to impermissible conduct. . . . When criminal violence occurs on the campus, university officials should promptly call for the assistance of law-enforcement agencies. When faced with disruptive but nonviolent conduct, the university should be prepared to respond initially with internal measures. . . . Faculty members who engage in or lead disruptive conduct have no place in the university community. . . .

University governance systems should be reformed to increase participation of students and faculty in the formulation of university policies that affect them. . . . Universities must become true communities whose members share a sense of respect, tolerance and responsibility for one another.

For law-enforcement agencies, the Commission had these recommendations:

Sending civil authorities to a college campus armed as if for war—armed only to kill—has brought tragedy in the past. If this practice is not changed, tragedy will come again. Shoulder weapons (except for tear-gas launchers) are very rarely needed on the campus; they should not be used except as emergency equipment in the face of sniper fire or armed resistance justifying them. We recommend that National Guardsmen receive much more training in controlling civil disturbances. . . . We urge that it [the Guard] have sufficient tactical capability and nonlethal weaponry so that it will use deadly force only as the absolute last resort.

In an interview granted when the Commission released its report in September 1970, Chairman Scranton said he felt that neither President Nixon nor his administration shared the Commission's sense of urgency about the problems discussed in the report. "Since last spring, up to this minute, there has not been the kind of leadership [needed] to bring about the kind of reconciliation that we're talking about," Scranton said. "The divisions are far deeper, far more compelling, and growing far faster than most Americans realize."

For eleven weeks after the release of the report, Nixon made no detailed comment on it. Then, in a letter to Scranton, the President took sharp issue with some of the Commission's chief recommendations. He thus placed himself in the position of repudiating to a large degree the findings of a panel he himself had appointed.

The President took particular issue with the Commission's view that it was up to him to heal the nation's divisions over social problems—especially those on the campus. "There are widely divergent views within our society as to just what our problems are," Nixon wrote Scranton. And no minority "has veto power over a President's decision to do what he believes is right in the nation's interest.

"Responsibility for maintaining a peaceful and open climate for learning in an academic community does not rest with the federal government—it rests squarely with the members of that academic community themselves. . . . Moral authority in a great nation such as ours does not reside in the presidency alone. There are thousands upon thousands of individuals—clergy, teachers, public officials, scholars, writers—to whom segments of the nation look for moral, intellectual and spiritual leadership."

The President pointed out that college students comprised 4 percent of the nation's population. "They have the right to be heard—both collectively and as individuals," he said. "Yet, no single group within a democratic society has a superior right to be heeded; and no single group has the right to use coercion, disruption or violence to achieve its political ends or social objectives."

In short, the President made clear he had little sympathy with the politics of confrontation. And his administration did little to implement the recommendations of the Scranton commission. The others addressed by the Commission—the students, the educators, the law-enforcement officers, and others—responded with varying degrees of enthusiasm or opposition to the recommendations. But there has been no visible sign that the nation is coming together in the manner suggested by the Commission.

Kent State and other examples of confrontation politics on campus have shown the vital forces that can be exerted for good or ill by students. Since the tragedy, perceptible changes have occurred at Kent State. Administrators say there has been a decisive shift to the left in the political thinking of many students. Junior faculty members have been demanding increased roles in determining university policies. The administration has made significant attempts to become more responsive to student needs—opening new lines of communication. At the same time, however, Ohio legislators have enacted measures—considered repressive by many students—to punish severely those who take part in campus disorders.

In the long view confrontation politics has been a vital force in effecting change on the nation's campuses. As a result of various confrontations, students now play more important roles in deciding on curriculum matters, in evaluating teacher performance, and, in a few cases, even in determining whether staff members will be hired or fired. Confrontation strategy has significantly expanded freedom of speech and freedom of the press on campuses. In general, students have gained a greater sense of control over the policies determining how they will be educated.

By and large, confrontation strategy has worked effectively on campus when students have been well-led and well-organized, when their demands have been related directly to issues on which the university can effect reforms, when such demands have been open to negotiation, and when emotionalism has been kept to a minimum. Confrontation strategy generally has been ineffective when it has escalated into campus violence, when university administrators or public officials have felt compelled to call in law-enforcement officers, and when student protests have dealt with issues beyond the jurisdiction of university officials (such as the Cambodia intervention).

The evidence seems clear that there is a place for confrontation politics on campus. But it must be practiced judiciously; it must not be allowed to become the sort of Russian roulette described by Irving Howe.

III
The Peace Movement

9

Antiwar Confrontations in the Nation's Capital

IN ADDITION to campus demonstrations, other protests against the war in Southeast Asia have offered some of the most dramatic examples of confrontation politics in recent history. These demonstrations included numerous mass marches in Washington and other cities across the country, attempts to seize government buildings, and efforts to cause such chaos in the nation's capital that the business of government would grind to a halt. In addition to such mass protests, there were countless episodes in which individuals or small groups confronted the establishment by burning draft cards in public, invading draft-board offices and destroying files, and committing other acts of defiance.

The antiwar movement brought together a seemingly strange coalition of persons of diverse backgrounds, ranging from black militant leader Stokely Carmichael to pediatrician Benjamin Spock, from white-haired grandmothers to long-haired hippies. And these divergent persons made common cause in the politics of confrontation.

One of the most widely publicized antiwar confrontations—Norman Mailer wrote a book about it, entitled *The*

Armies of the Night—was an attempt by groups of peace demonstrators to invade the Pentagon in October 1967. Although highly organized, with volunteer monitors placed at strategic points in the crowd to maintain discipline, the demonstration was doomed from the start to fail in its announced purpose. The demonstrators had no more chance of getting past the Military Policemen and federal marshals stationed around the headquarters of the U.S. Defense Department than they had of achieving one of their other supposed goals—levitating the building off the ground. The attempted invasion of the Pentagon had been announced long in advance, so there was no question of taking the government by surprise. And since the target was a building containing more of this country's military secrets than any other, the security was so tight that even a heavily armed corps of invaders would have faced a hopeless task. Still, the unarmed demonstrators made their attempt and were turned back. Many were arrested, convicted of a variety of crimes, and sentenced to jail.

What purpose did the confrontation serve, if it was obvious beforehand that the demonstrators could not attain their goal? The participants contended that their very attempt, unsuccessful as it was bound to be, would demonstrate the deep commitment of many Americans to the campaign to end the war. They pointed out that although there were many hippies, Yippies, and other radical types among the protesters, large contingents of highly respected Americans were also involved—including such men as author Mailer, poet Robert Lowell, literary critic Dwight Macdonald, and Dr. Spock. It was argued that the prestige they lent the confrontation gave it an air of respectability. The hope was that the Pentagon demonstration would inspire numerous other confrontations in protest of the war.

In fact, a wave of antiwar protests did follow the march

on the Pentagon. Some were orderly, some disruptive. Opponents of the demonstrations tried to discredit them by claiming that they had been organized largely by communists. For example, Chairman Edwin E. Willis of the U.S. House Committee on Un-American Activities charged that "the Communist party, U.S.A., and other communist organizations and their adherents have been importantly involved in the great majority of [antiwar rallies] and have been the originating and guiding force in the major demonstrations." Other observers, however, contended that while some communists undoubtedly were involved in the peace movement, their numbers were few and their influence was small.

If the charges of communist manipulation bothered the many thousands of non-communist peace activists, they didn't show it. In fact, their participation in antiwar confrontations seemed to increase markedly after the charges by Willis and other critics of the peace movement. Little purpose would be served by recounting in detail a great number of these demonstrations; suffice it to say that hundreds of them took place in various cities during the late 1960s and early 1970s. But for purposes of comparison it seems appropriate to examine two particular protests that were staged in the nation's capital within a period of several weeks—one entirely orderly and the other intentionally disruptive.

On April 24, 1971, more than two hundred thousand antiwar demonstrators from all sections of the country gathered in Washington to urge President Nixon and the Congress to bring an immediate end to the war in Southeast Asia. Having assembled behind the White House, they marched, in an orderly demonstration that lasted for more than three hours because of the enormity of the crowd, to the steps of the U.S. Capitol Building. There they heard a succession of speakers, including members of the House of Representatives and the Senate, argue passionately in behalf of pulling U.S. troops out of Indochina. Among the speakers were Mrs. Coretta Scott King, widow of the assassinated Dr. Martin Luther King, Jr.; the Reverend Ralph Abernathy, King's successor as head of the Southern Christian Leadership Conference; former Navy lieutenant John F. Kerry, a spokesman for a thousand antiwar veterans of the Vietnam war; Louis Font, a West Point graduate who had been released from the Army as a conscientious objector; and numerous leaders of labor unions and other organizations.

One labor leader—David Livingston, president of District 65 of the National Retail Distributive Workers Union—told the crowd: "We would like for the whole world to know why we are meeting here—to appeal to the House of Representatives and the Senate and to say to them, 'Under the Constitution, you can end the war.'" Congressman Herman Badillo of New York, who followed Livingston to the podium, assured the demonstrators, "You have come to the right place." And Congresswoman Bella Abzug, also of New York, said, "Your presence here today means that you're going to force Congress to undeclare this war."

The demonstration did not quite do that. But protesters who remained in Washington after the rally to speak with Congressmen and Senators found generally warm welcomes awaiting them. Although some Congressmen and Senators did not agree with their positions on the war, they were virtually unanimous in applauding the peaceful and responsible way in which the demonstrators had made their views known. It would not be overstating the case to say that the behavior of these protesters helped create a more favorable climate in Congress for proposed measures aimed at ending the war.

Little more than a week later, however, this climate was jeopardized by the disruptive tactics of other demonstrators, who had come to Washington following the Capitol rally. In the forefront of these new demonstrators were members of the Mayday Tribe, an organization headed by a group of young radical leaders that included Rennie Davis, a nationally known veteran of many protest movements, and Steven D'Arazien, a former official of Students for a Democratic Society.

The Mayday Tribe, in a "tactical manual" distributed to prospective demonstrators, described its strategy in these terms: "Thousands of us with bamboo flutes, tambourines, flowers and balloons moving out in the early light of morning to paralyze the traffic arteries of the American military repression government nerve center. Creativeness, joy and life against bureaucracy and grim death. That's nonviolent civil disobedience; that's Mayday. . . . The aim of the Mayday actions is to raise the social cost of the war to a level unacceptable to America's rulers. To do this we seek to create the specter of social chaos while maintaining the support or at least toleration of the broad masses of American people."

Stripped of its verbiage, the Mayday Tribe's plan called for supposedly nonviolent hit-and-run guerrilla tactics on the streets of Washington and the bridges leading into the capital from Virginia and Maryland—all designed to cause such monumental traffic jams that government workers would be unable to reach their offices. The absence of the workers, Mayday claimed, would cause the machinery of government to grind to a standstill.

On May 3, shortly before the morning traffic rush began, demonstrators fanned out through the Washington area. Awaiting them were large contingents of police and federal troops. As cars began making their way into downtown

Washington, the demonstrators did their best to block the streets—with piles of trash, tree limbs, bricks, lumber, nails, bottles, stones, garbage cans, and parked vehicles—and to harass the drivers. Moving in groups as small as ten and as large as a hundred they sat down in the middle of roads and bridges, paced in and out among stalled cars, and generally tried to create chaos. The police and federal troops kept constantly on the move, trying to break up the demonstrations. In many sections of the city tear gas was fired. At other points, despite the claims by the Mayday leaders that the protest was to be nonviolent, there were clashes between demonstrators and policemen and soldiers.

In the end, law-enforcement officers resorted to dragnet arrests in many cases arresting bystanders merely because of their long hair or their clothing. All told, more than 7,000 persons were arrested—the highest arrest total for a single day in Washington history. About 150 protesters and 5 policemen were injured seriously enough to need hospital treatment.

The demonstration failed to come close to achieving its purpose. Although many workers were delayed in reaching their offices, all arrived in time to put in close to a full day's work. Nonetheless, the protest leaders decided to continue applying pressure on the government. New demonstrations were conducted the following day, and 2,680 more protesters were arrested. The day after that an attempt was made to invade the House of Representatives and disrupt the operations of Congress. A line of helmeted policemen hurled back the demonstrators, and another 1,146 persons were arrested.

The tactics of the Mayday Tribe undid much of the goodwill in Congress that had been engendered by the orderly peace demonstration of April 24. Although substantial numbers of Congressmen and Senators deplored the dragnet-arrest methods used to break up the Mayday Tribe demonstrations, accusing President Nixon and Attorney General John Mitchell of ordering repressive measures, their revulsion over the methods used by the Mayday protesters was even greater.

In the end, many of the charges filed against the Mayday demonstrators and the innocent bystanders were dismissed. There had been such confusion among the law-enforcement officers at the time of the arrests that it was impossible for individual policemen to testify about specific illegal acts purportedly committed by those arrested. The dismissal of the charges reinforced the position of those who accused the Nixon administration and the police of repressive activities.

Later in this book, there will be further discussion of other confrontation tactics employed by peace activists and an evaluation of the effects of such tactics. As for the April 24 and Mayday demonstrations, it seems clear that the earlier protest was a success and the later one a failure. The April 24 demonstration was well-organized and highly disciplined, and had a clearly defined goal: using the force of public opinion to influence government leaders. The Mayday demonstrations were poorly organized and undisciplined, and had a dubious goal: disruption for disruption's sake. Even if they had succeeded in bringing the machinery of government to a standstill, there is no reason to believe this would have produced an early end to the war. The Mayday demonstrations were not directed at appropriate targets. They did not affect government leaders with power to end the war so much as they did ordinary citizens who wanted only to be left alone as they made their way to work. Thus, the demonstrations accomplished little except the creation of new antagonism toward the antiwar movement—much of it among private citizens and public officials who had previously tended to support measures designed to end the war.

The April 24 and Mayday protests provided fresh evidence that confrontation tactics can be effective when used judiciously, but can do more harm than good when used irresponsibly.

IV
Confronting the Political Process

10

Disruptions at the Republican and Democratic National Conventions

FOR the most part, the targets of confrontation politics are public institutions, government officials, or specific government policies. Occasionally, however, confrontations are aimed at changing the course of the political process itself. Such was the case in 1968 when confrontations were staged in attempts to influence both the Democratic and Republican national conventions.

The disruptions at the Democratic convention in Chicago received such wide attention that many casual observers have forgotten there were also disorders attending the Republican convention in Miami Beach. The Republican convention took place during the week of August 5, three weeks before the Democratic convention. Florida officials, who had been trying to lure the Democratic gathering to Miami Beach along with the Republican convention, had argued for weeks that the probability of troublesome demonstrations would be far lower in their state than in Illinois, the other site being considered by the Democrats. Although the Democrats ultimately decided to stage their convention in Chicago, these assurances from Florida officials were resented by black leaders who had long and unsuccessfully tried to improve conditions in Miami's black neighborhoods. The wide advertisement of local blacks' supposedly passive attitudes was, they felt, demeaning to the black community and false in its implication that the black community was content with its economic and social lot. What better way to counteract these impressions than by staging some sort of confrontation at the Republican convention? National political figures, leading black activists from throughout the country, and huge contingents from the news media all would be on hand for the convention. Here would be a golden opportunity to draw national attention to conditions in local ghetto neighborhoods.

Just before the opening of the Republican convention, local black leaders met and decided to call a mass rally for August 7. At the rally, a protest would be organized against various all-white state delegations to the Republican convention. In addition, demands would be made for black economic and political control of ghetto areas, guaranteed annual incomes, black policemen and firemen in black neighborhoods, and other reforms. From the rally, participants were expected to drive to the site of the Republican convention, seven miles away, and continue their protest.

Among those listed by the sponsors as scheduled speakers at the rally were basketball star Wilt Chamberlain and the Reverend Ralph Abernathy. When the rally started, however, neither Chamberlain nor Abernathy appeared. (Both later said they had not promised to attend.) The meeting room where the rally was held was too small to accommodate the several hundred persons who showed up, so part of the crowd overflowed into the street and listened to the speeches over loudspeakers. Many of those outside the meeting room were teen-agers, angry because Wilt Chamberlain had not appeared and fired up by the speeches and the literature distributed at the rally. Venting their frustrations on the closest tangible targets, they began throwing stones at passing motorists and shouting insults at policemen assigned to the area, which was known as Liberty City.

Gradually the disturbances grew in intensity. Assaults were made on policemen. Additional squads of officers rushed to the scene, and hundreds more blacks surged into the streets from apartment houses in the neighborhood. Over a period of more than six hours, the disruptions escalated until they constituted a full-scale riot. Black youths went on a rampage through the neighborhood, looting and vandalizing stores. Police eventually used tear gas to gain control of the area.

Public officials, including Miami Mayor Steve Clark and Florida Governor Claude Kirk, came to Liberty City that night and met with black leaders to discuss their grievances. Further meetings were scheduled for succeeding days. But when the officials failed to appear for the promised meetings, new disturbances erupted. Looting was resumed, several buildings were set on fire, and crowds of blacks surrounded officers sent to restore order.

At one point sniper fire was reported by police. Officers fired warning shots from automatic rifles and shotguns to disperse the crowds. But then, as demonstrators scurried for cover, some officers continued firing their weapons— aiming at the blacks. The shooting lasted for several minutes. By the time it ended, two black civilians—both adults —had been shot to death. A black child had been wounded by the gunfire. Several policemen had been injured, not by gunfire but by thrown objects. Eventually, Governor Kirk sent 950 National Guardsmen to reinforce the police in the riot area, but still the disturbances continued.

In another shooting incident, one black man was killed by the police, three others were seriously wounded, and nine received relatively minor wounds. Still later another black man was shot to death by an officer. It was not until August 13—six days after the initial disturbances—that the violence ended and law enforcement officers withdrew from the Liberty City area.

It is fair to say that poor planning for the August 7 rally contributed to the atmosphere that led to the violence. Selection of a meeting room too small to accommodate even a moderate-sized crowd forced many of the demonstrators into the streets, where no provisions had been made for maintaining discipline. The false promise that Wilt Chamberlain and the Reverend Ralph Abernathy would appear added to the discontent and helped set the stage for the disturbances. Beyond that, black leaders seem to have had no clear, detailed program for their protests. And they lacked control over their supporters. When the violence erupted, the black leaders were able to exert little influence in trying to restore order.

Although the original rally had been prompted by factors related to the Republican convention, the ensuing disturbances at no point intruded directly on the Republican convention. And after the initial riot that followed the rally, there was no clear indication that those involved in the disruptions hoped to influence the convention.

Moreover, despite the rhetoric and violence in Liberty City—despite the four deaths and the many injuries—the protests seem to have had no appreciable effect on the Republican convention. No all-white delegations were integrated because of the confrontations. No dramatic changes in the Party's platform were adopted. And the candidates nominated at the convention, Richard Nixon for President and Spiro Agnew for Vice-President, gave no indications during the subsequent campaign that the confrontations had affected their policies. All in all, it must be concluded

CONFRONTING THE POLITICAL PROCESS   131

that the Miami protests accomplished few of their objectives.

In contrast with the Miami disturbances, the confrontations that occurred during the Democrat convention in Chicago were much more directly connected with the political meeting itself. The circumstances leading to these demonstrations had been long in the making. Almost five months before the Democrats convened, President Lyndon B. Johnson had announced that he would neither seek nor accept the Democratic nomination for reelection. At the time of his announcement, Johnson's policy of continuing the war in Southeast Asia was under sharp attack, and many peace activists were gearing up for a major effort to nominate a Democratic candidate pledged to end the war. Senator Eugene McCarthy of Minnesota was seeking the Presidential nomination on a peace platform, with the support of many young people opposed to the war. After McCarthy made a strong showing in the New Hampshire primary, Senator Robert Kennedy also entered the race for the nomination, basing his campaign largely on the peace issue.

With Johnson out of the race, Vice-President Hubert Humphrey inherited from the President the support of many old-line "regular" Democratic leaders. In that position, and since he was serving as Vice-President while seeking the Presidency, Humphrey seemed obliged to support in at least general terms the Johnson program in Southeast Asia—including continuation of the war until an "honorable settlement" had been reached. After the assassination of Senator Kennedy, Humphrey became the clear-cut favorite to win the nomination.

Many of the peace activists who had planned to oppose President Johnson's renomination shifted their opposition to Humphrey. In advance of the convention, various activist groups began planning a series of confrontations in Chicago aimed at demonstrating opposition to the Johnson-Humphrey administration and pressuring the Democrats into adopting a platform that called for an early end to the war.

Foremost among the organizations seeking to form a coalition for united action was the National Mobilization Committee to End the War in Vietnam. The Committee, which had previously organized the attempt to invade the Pentagon and other antiwar protests, was headed by David Dellinger, editor of a publication called *Liberation*. Working closely with Dellinger were such left-wing leaders as Rennie Davis, head of the Center for Radical Research, and Tom Hayden, a former president of Students for a Democratic Society and a major theoretician of the New Left.

Among the many groups that cooperated with the National Mobilization Committee in planning the confrontation strategy were: The Youth International Party, commonly known as the Yippies, whose leaders included such well-known radicals as Abbie Hoffman, Jerry Rubin, and Paul Krassner; Youth Against War and Fascism, a militant extremist organization; the Vietnam Peace Parade Committee, a New York antiwar organization; the Cleveland Area Peace Action Committee; the Chicago Peace Council; the Legal Defense Committee, organized by Chicago attorneys, and the National Lawyers Guild, both of which were assigned to provide legal aid to demonstrators who might be arrested; the Communist Party; the Progressive Labor Party; the Young Socialist Party; and several religious organizations.

With such divergent groups involved, numerous conflicts of interest were bound to arise. The Yippies centered their plans around an event to be called a Festival of Life—a supposedly spontaneous outpouring of joy that would take place among thousands of young people camping out in a Chicago park. They also had a program that included—in addition to ending the war—the legalizing of psychedelic drugs and the abolition of money, "pay housing, pay media, pay transportation, pay food, pay education, pay clothing, pay medical help and pay toilets." Some of the more serious leaders of the Chicago coalition tended to view the Yippies' planned activities as frivolous. Rennie Davis, for one, said, "I think that my reaction to the Festival of Life . . . was . . . that it was *very important* that that not come to be too important in the public mind or in the Movement's mind."

The planning of the Chicago demonstrations had been underway for about a year before the Democrat convention. At various times during that year, leaders of the protest had seriously talked about mounting organized disruptions that would interfere with the Democrat delegates' business at the convention. At one planning session the leaders considered creating such disruption that the convention would be forced to shut down. At another session, Tom Hayden said, "We should have people organized who can fight the police, people who are willing to get arrested. . . . My thinking is not to leave the initiative to the police. We don't want to get into the trap of violence versus passive action."

Ultimately, however, Rennie Davis claims, it was decided that while it was appropriate to try to disrupt activities at the Pentagon, it would not be appropriate to use disruptive tactics at the convention. "Our clear decision that it was not valid to disrupt the convention was based on the fact that we realized that if we transferred our attention from the Pentagon to the convention there would be a shift in the kind of institution we were confronting," Davis said. "And whereas there is a pretty unanimous agreement that the

Pentagon is *per se* an evil institution and therefore we felt quite prepared to call for disruption of the Pentagon, for shutting it down, the convention itself was not an evil institution *per se*."

At a meeting on August 4, three weeks before the opening of the convention, protest leaders agreed on a program of demonstrations proposed by Davis. His scenario included picketing on August 25 by antiwar groups in front of the Hilton Hotel, where many of the convention delegates would be staying; an "anti-birthday party" for President Johnson on August 27, when the convention was expected to observe his birthday; a mass march, on August 28, to the site of the convention, the International Amphitheatre, where demonstrators would "hold a vigil, create [street] theater and rally for as long as the convention lasts"; and a series of smaller, decentralized protests throughout convention week. On the surface, at least, these protests did not seem destined to cause serious disturbances. But there had been so much talk in previous months about the possibility of violence at the convention that many of those involved in the upcoming events—Democratic delegates, police, city officials, and demonstrators alike—came to expect trouble.

This expectation led Senator Eugene McCarthy to urge thousands of his youthful supporters, who had been counted upon to swell the ranks of the demonstrators, to stay away from Chicago. Many of McCarthy's young backers did stay away as a result of the request, but many others went through with their original plans to join the demonstrations.

Many of the demonstrations planned could not be conducted legally without permits from the city of Chicago. Protest leaders engaged in extensive negotiations with city officials to obtain such permits, but the two sides could not agree on times, places, and other conditions. Ultimately the

CONFRONTING THE POLITICAL PROCESS 135

National Mobilization Committee filed suit seeking a court order requiring the city to grant certain permits. The suit was thrown out of court. New negotiations ensued and the city finally granted one permit, allowing an afternoon rally in Grant Park on August 27. The permit was conditional on the Committee's obtaining a large liability-insurance policy in advance of the rally. The policy was never obtained, so technically the permit never took effect.

The Yippies initially sought a permit to allow the thousands of young people expected at their Festival of Life to sleep in Lincoln Park. When the permit was denied, the Yippies filed suit to obtain it, but eventually withdrew the suit and decided to go ahead with the plans anyway. They assumed that once thousands of demonstrators set up camp in the park, the city would at least informally waive the permit requirement.

In preparation for the expected demonstrations, extensive security precautions had been taken by Chicago police and other law-enforcement agencies, including the Secret Service (responsible for protecting the President, Vice-President, and candidates for those offices), the National Guard, military intelligence units, and private firms employed by the Democratic National Committee to handle security problems. Indications are that at least some members of the Chicago police force, aware for months of the rumors that there would be violence at the convention, were ready to "crack some heads" at the first sign of civil disorder.

Police antagonism toward the protesters was aggravated by events in the days immediately preceding the convention. As demonstrators arrived in Chicago, protest leaders gave them detailed instruction (often under the eyes of television news cameras) in techniques to be used in confrontations with the police. One technique that drew great attention, both from newsmen and the police, was the *washoi*, a maneuver borrowed from student demonstrations in Japan. In the *washoi* groups of marchers line up ten to twenty persons across and as deep as possible, linking arms and holding each other's waists. They then move forward, backward, or sideways in unison, with their maneuvers resembling the movements of a snake. When the *washoi* was taught in Lincoln Park, it presented a fearsome spectacle that undoubtedly led some policemen to assume the demonstrators would be looking for trouble. Actually, protest leaders contended, the *washoi* was merely a device for moving a group out of a riot situation without causing or sustaining injury. Instructions were also given, however, in karate and judo.

The first serious violence of the pre-convention period occurred on August 22 a few blocks southwest of Lincoln Park. For some reason that has never been satisfactorily explained, a seventeen-year-old American Indian identified as a member of the Yippies opened fire on several Chicago policemen with a .32-caliber revolver. The police returned the fire and the youth, Jerome Johnson of Sioux Falls, South Dakota, was shot to death. The shooting caused one protest leader to say, "We don't want to go overboard in ascribing malevolent intentions to the police, but obviously things are going to be getting very rough here. We've got to be prepared."

It was not long before things did indeed begin "getting very rough." Between August 22 and August 25, demonstrators and policemen engaged in various minor confrontations. A few arrests were made, but no major violence occurred. Then, on the night of August 25, with many of the Democratic delegates already in Chicago, the demonstrators stepped up their activities, and serious violence did erupt. Earlier in the day there had been a series of confrontations in Lincoln Park between the police and demonstrators, many of them Yippies and their supporters. The police had broken up a variety of protest gatherings.

Demonstrators, shouting obscenities and antiwar slogans, had taunted the police throughout the afternoon. In retaliation, the police had started handling the protesters roughly, though not brutally. Some of the officers had taken off their badges and nameplates, presumably to make it harder for demonstrators to identify them in case the situation grew more violent.

Shortly after 8:30 P.M., about twenty protesters surrounded a dozen officers and backed them up against the wall of a fieldhouse in the park. The demonstrators shouted abuse at them. As the protesters' ranks grew, they began throwing small rocks and lighted cigarettes at the officers.

For a half hour the police did not retaliate. They merely stood silently, glaring at the protesters. Then, with only a brief shout of "Get out of the way," the police charged fiercely at the demonstrators, swinging their clubs at anyone they could reach. Many of those in the crowd, who claimed they had merely been watching the confrontation, were clubbed to the ground and beaten. The scene was described by a volunteer medic from the Northwestern University Medical School: "When someone would fall, three or four cops would start beating him. One kid was beaten so badly he couldn't get up. He was bleeding profusely from the head. The kids scattered to the street as the police moved about two hundred yards and then regrouped around the building. A couple of dozen Yippies were clubbed. I treated five myself." This medic said he saw another medic, wearing a white coat, struck by an officer. When the second medic yelled, "I'm a medic," the officer replied, "Excuse me." Then the officer clubbed him again.

From that point on, the civil disorder and violence in Chicago mounted steadily. As the authorities tried to clear

Lincoln Park, demonstrators by the thousands swarmed through the streets, disrupting traffic and causing havoc. Police retaliated with devastating sweeps through the streets, attacking demonstrators, newsmen, innocent bystanders, even some Democratic convention delegates who got caught in the turmoil. Skirmishes continued throughout the convention week. These confrontations have been the subject of wide publicity and discussion, and thus need not be described in detail here. Suffice it to say that never had such widespread violence attended any previous political convention in the nation's history.

All told, Chicago policemen arrested 668 persons. Most of those arrested were twenty-six years of age or younger, came from the Chicago area, and had no prior arrest records. About 47 percent of the defendants came from outside the Chicago area. They included persons from thirty-six states, the District of Columbia, and five foreign countries.

The police reported that 192 officers had been injured during the week-long violence. Statistics on injuries among civilians were not nearly so precise, but the best estimate was that about 1,025 civilians were treated at hospitals, special medical facilities set up for the demonstrations, and mobile field stations.

The National Commission on the Causes and Prevention of Violence, appointed by President Johnson after the assassinations of Dr. Martin Luther King, Jr., and Senator Robert Kennedy, named a study team to investigate the Chicago confrontations. The team was headed by Daniel Walker, president of the Chicago Crime Commission. It produced a lengthy report on the convention-week violence, entitled *Rights in Conflict*, that was highly critical of Chicago Mayor Richard Daley and the Chicago police force.

The report's chief finding was that a "police riot" erupted

in Chicago. It concluded that at times the police acted not merely with "unrestrained and indiscriminate" violence but with "ferocity" in attempts to repress dissent. Some of the police conduct, the report said, was "malicious or mindless." It said that police not only clubbed many innocent persons, but also took part in some confrontations in which "the weight of the violence was overwhelmingly on the side of the police."

In placing a major share of the blame on Mayor Daley, the study team pointed out that earlier he had been critical of the police for their supposed restraint in handling the disorders that followed the assassination of Dr. King. After those disorders, Daley had ordered police to "shoot to kill arsonists and shoot to maim looters." The study team concluded that the mayor's get-tough policy had encouraged local officers to engage in the police riot during convention week.

The study team did not absolve demonstrators of blame. It pointed out that "the Chicago police were the targets of mounting provocation by both word and act." The provocation, the report said, included "obscene epithets and rocks, sticks, bathroom tiles and even human feces hurled at police by demonstrators." Some of these acts had been planned, others were spontaneous, and still others were provoked by police action, the report noted. It said that some acts of confrontation were instigated by revolutionaries, but concluded: "Despite the presence of some revolutionaries, the vast majority of the demonstrators were intent on expressing by peaceful means their dissent either from society generally or from the administration's policies in Vietnam."

What were the political repercussions of the Chicago confrontations? The question will be debated for years, but certain facts seem to have emerged clearly. The protests did not materially affect the outcome of the nomination process itself. Vice-President Hubert Humphrey was the clear-cut favorite for the Democratic Presidential nomination before the violence erupted, and he won the nomination. Nor did the confrontations persuade the convention to adopt a strong antiwar plank in the Party's platform. They were, however, considered at least partly responsible for Democratic Party reforms which led to major increases in the number of women, young people, blacks and members of other minorities among the delegates to the 1972 Democratic convention.

During the 1968 election campaign—perhaps partly in response to the antiwar protests in Chicago—Hubert Humphrey did move cautiously away from the precise war policy advocated by President Johnson. But he did not move nearly so far as the antiwar movement wanted. The Chicago violence proved to be an albatross around Humphrey's neck in his campaign against Richard Nixon for the Presidency. Nixon and his running mate, Spiro Agnew, campaigning hard on the "law and order" theme, were able to make great political capital out of the Chicago disorders. Some qualified observers believe the events in Chicago doomed the Humphrey candidacy; that, had they not occurred, he would have been elected President.

Other observers point to the Chicago confrontations as a turning point in this country's political history. They contend that the Chicago violence and the revulsion over the police tactics have radicalized many of those involved in politics. While there has been a discernible shift to the left among some prominent political figures since the 1968 convention, these claims seem over-stated.

Over the long haul, the most significant effects of the Chicago disorders on the history of confrontation politics may stem from the prosecution of seven of the protest leaders on federal conspiracy and riot charges. In March 1969 a federal grand jury in Chicago returned the first indictment handed down under a new anti-riot law passed in 1968. Named as defendants were David Dellinger, Rennie Davis, Tom Hayden, Abbie Hoffman, Jerry Rubin, Lee Weiner (a sociology teacher at Northwestern University who had helped plan the Chicago demonstrations), John Froines (a chemistry professor at the University of Oregon who also participated in the planning), and Bobby Seale, a founder of the Black Panther Party. (During the trial, Seale was ordered bound and gagged for insisting, against the judge's orders, on trying to represent himself and question witnesses. The judge held him in contempt, sentenced him to four years—only to have the sentence upset by an appeals court—and separated Seale's case from that of the other defendants. Eventually the conspiracy and riot charges against Seale were dismissed. Because of the severance of his case from that of the others, the group, which had become known as the "Chicago Eight," was reduced to the "Chicago Seven.")

As in the case of the Chicago confrontations themselves, the trial of the "Chicago Seven" received such wide publicity that it does not require detailed discussion here. But the legal framework on which the prosecution was based does deserve discussion because of the broad impact it may have on the politics of confrontation.

The indictment in the case was brought under a section of the 1968 anti-riot law that makes it a federal crime to travel in interstate commerce or use any facility of interstate commerce (such as a telephone) with the intention of inciting, promoting, encouraging, participating in, or carrying on a riot. The law defines a riot as any assembly of three or more persons in which at least one person threatens injury to another person or property or actually injures someone or some property.

In the Chicago Seven case the grand jury accused the defendants of conspiring to travel in interstate commerce with the intent "to incite, organize, promote, encourage, participate in and carry on a riot" as barred by the law, teach and demonstrate to other persons "the use of incendiary devices which may obstruct, delay and adversely affect commerce," and "commit acts to obstruct, impede and interfere with firemen and law-enforcement officers . . . and adversely affect commerce."

The trial degenerated into a circus in which vitriolic remarks were frequently exchanged between the defendants and their lawyers and Federal District Judge Julius Hoffman. A jury convicted Dellinger, Hayden, Abbie Hoffman, Davis, and Rubin of crossing state lines to incite a riot, but found Weiner and Froines not guilty. All the defendants were found not guilty on the conspiracy charge. Judge Hoffman ruled that all the defendants, including Weiner and Froines, had been guilty of contempt of court, and gave them all jail sentences. In addition, he held defense attorneys William Kunstler and Leonard Weinglass in contempt and handed them jail terms. All the contempt sentences were later ruled invalid by a higher court. The convictions on the riot charges were also upset on appeal.

Various legal experts—including Ramsey Clark, who was U.S. attorney general at the time the 1968 anti-riot law was passed—contend that the anti-riot law is unconstitutional. It does not take much imagination to fathom how a repressive national administration intent on curbing dissent could misuse the anti-riot law. Any protest in which three or more persons assembled and in which some threat was voiced against a person or property could be construed as a riot. And one telephone call across state lines in planning a protest would give federal prosecutors the hook they needed to file criminal charges.

One of the more controversial questions arising from the Chicago demonstrations and other antiwar confrontations is how well they have succeeded in accomplishing their goals. Some observers claim confrontations have produced substantial results. They say that antiwar protests influenced President Johnson's decision not to seek reelection; helped reduce, at least for a time, American bombing strikes in Southeast Asia; speeded the decision to withdraw American ground troops from Vietnam; mobilized public opinion against the war; pressed Congress into trying to assume greater responsibility over foreign affairs; attracted "respectable" people into the peace movement, and finally led to a cease-fire.

Other observers argue that these results might have come about even in the absence of antiwar confrontations; that they might have been produced by the sheer length of the war, the heavy casualties, the resulting disillusionment on the part of the American people, and the leadership of such antiwar politicians as George McGovern, Eugene McCarthy, and the late Robert Kennedy.

Still others contend that the antiwar confrontations failed to achieve their purpose. They maintain that the cease-fire was unrelated to the antiwar protests. They insist it was the result of a new willingness by the Vietnamese communists to end the hostilities. These observers argue that President Nixon pursued a Vietnam policy not markedly different from President Johnson's. Nixon showed no tendency, on the surface at least, to be moved by antiwar confrontations. Moreover, some experts maintain, antiwar confrontations may bring about a long-range curbing of dissent in this country. They point to the fact that the 1968 federal anti-riot law was passed partly in response to the wave of antiwar protests that swept the nation. If that law compromises future dissent, they argue, the antiwar confrontations will be at least partly to blame.

The final word on the long-range impact of antiwar confrontations will have to be left to future historians. In the meantime, those involved in the politics of confrontation are faced with eventful choices.

V
The Resort to Terrorism

11

Bombers, Snipers, and Arsonists

A RECENT development in the history of confrontation politics has been the resort to terrorist tactics. The number of bombings, sniper attacks, ambushes of policemen, and other assaults on persons and property committed in the name of some political cause has risen drastically in the past few years. Revolutionaries, patterning themselves after such "heroes" as Ché Guevara, have roamed the country on guerrilla missions. Often other protesters have inaccurately been branded as members, associates, or supporters of terrorist groups.

There is a question whether an act such as a bombing, carried out in secret, is a legitimate example of confrontation politics. After all, the dictionary defines *confrontation* as "the act of facing in hostility or defiance." Since a person or group carrying out a clandestine bombing does not actually come face to face with an adversary, it can be argued that such an act does qualify as an instance of confrontation politics. On the other hand, those who engage in politically inspired bombings often do seek to confront the establishment by telephoning clues about their identities to the news media or the police, in effect advertising their crimes and daring law-enforcement agencies to catch them. Moreover, such bombings themselves—while carried out in secret—are usually intended to change the political system by confronting it with violence. Thus, for purposes of this book, they will be considered acts of political confrontation.

A few statistics illustrate the prevalence of bombings in America today: During one fifteen-month period, the country suffered 4,330 bombings resulting in 43 deaths and $21.8 million in property damage. In addition, there were 1,175 attempted bombings and 35,129 bomb threats.

No section of the country has been immune from this host of explosions. Among the bombers' targets have been the U.S. Capitol Building, an ROTC building at the University of California at Santa Barbara, four electric-transmission towers owned by the Public Service Company of Colorado, a Slovak civic club in Cleveland, a building on the campus of Rutgers University in New Jersey, the home of a black who instituted a school-integration suit in Denver, the Louisiana State Capitol Building, the headquarters of the New York City Police Department, and a mathematics research center at the University of Wisconsin.

Who are the militants engaged in this drastic form of confrontation politics? If their own claims and the claims of law-enforcement agencies are to be believed, many of them are members of a group called the Weathermen—an ultraradical faction of Students for a Democratic Society. And the most radical of the Weathermen, those most favoring violence, are said to belong to an elite corps known as the Weather Bureau. (The Weathermen take their name from a line in a Bob Dylan song, "Subterranean Homesick Blues": "You don't need a weatherman to know which way the wind blows." Another line in the song—"The pump don't work 'cause the vandals took the handles"—has been adopted by some Weathermen as a creed of sorts. As one of them put it, "That's what we're all about—being vandals in the mother country.")

Just what are the Weathermen all about? What are they trying to accomplish? And how are they going about it?

Their political theory was outlined in a lengthy position paper published in 1969. The paper began with the premise that all political strategy in this country must allow for the fact of American economic imperialism: "We are within the heartland of a worldwide monster, a country so rich from its worldwide plunder that even the crumbs doled out to the enslaved masses within its borders provide for material existence very much above the conditions of the masses of the people of the world."

The position paper contended that a worldwide revolution was in progress against American imperialism. The revolution was being fought, it argued, by the "Third World" peoples of Asia, Africa, and Latin America. In the United States—which the paper called "the mother country"—the revolution was said to involve chiefly the "black colony." The paper urged that white activists "get on the right side" of the revolution by joining with blacks in a struggle to smash the U.S. government. This smashing (a favorite Weatherman word) would be accomplished through a variety of guerrilla-style confrontations.

Although the position paper did not spell out all the Weathermen's tactics in detail, later events disclosed that bombing was one of their chief techniques. Another was the deliberate provocation of fist-fights between young radicals and their contemporaries in other segments of society—"straight" high-school students, for example, or tough working-class school dropouts. The purpose of these fights was to impress outsiders with the radicals' toughness and thus gain their respect, and, it was hoped, line up potential recruits. Still another technique was the staging of raids on bastions of the establishment, including public schools. In one such raid in Brooklyn, New York, Weathermen burst into a school, bound and gagged two teachers, and distributed leaflets claiming they were part of a "big gang" all over the country that intended to turn the United States into a communist nation.

But bombing has been the tactic that has chiefly set the Weathermen apart from many other protest organizations. In July 1970 a federal grand jury in Detroit indicted thirteen members of the Weathermen on charges of conspiracy to commit bombings in Detroit, Chicago, New York, and Berkeley. Among the defendants were Mark Rudd, the former leader of SDS at Columbia University; Kathy Boudin, daughter of a prominent civil-liberties lawyer; Cathlyn Platt Wilkerson, whose parents' town house in New York had apparently been used as a bomb factory and had accidentally been blown up four months before the indictment; and Bernardine Rae Dohrn, a leader of the Weather Bureau and former interorganizational secretary of SDS.

Justice Department officials said the investigation leading to the indictment was begun after the explosion at the Wilkersons' town house. The indictment charged that several of the defendants were in the house, "where dynamite bombs were assembled," at the time of the explosion. Two Weathermen, Ted Gold and Diana Oughton, were killed in the blast, and a third, Terry Robbins, was believed killed, although his body was never positively identified in the rubble. Miss Wilkerson and Miss Boudin were reported to have survived the explosion and gone into hiding.

The indictment charged the thirteen defendants, along with fifteen other persons who were named as co-conspirators but not indicted, with conspiring to "use bombs, destructive devices and explosives to destroy police installations and other civic, business and educational buildings throughout the country and to kill and injure persons therein." It stated that the defendants had agreed to organize a "central committee" to direct bombing operations, with various sections of the committee assigned to Chicago, Detroit, New York, and Berkeley. In addition, the indictment charged, they had decided to establish "clandestine and underground 'focals,' consisting of three or four persons," which would be under the command of the central committee and would carry out the bombings.

Members of the focals, the grand jury charged, would "travel throughout the country, using false identities and communication through coded messages, and purchase and obtain by other means weapons, firearms and dynamite and other explosives, fuses, detonating caps and other equipment for assembling explosive and incendiary bombs and destructive devices." The indictment cited twenty-one overt acts that one or more of the defendants was accused of committing to further the purported conspiracy.

The first such act allegedly occurred at a meeting in Flint, Michigan, where Mark Rudd was reported to have told various Weathermen they should take part in "bombings of police stations and banks throughout the country and the killing of police to further the revolution." Other overt acts charged in the indictment included specific cases in which the defendants supposedly concealed bombs, weapons, and ammunition in several cities, plotted bombings, and discussed assassination of policemen and others.

Various defendants in the case have remained in hiding ever since the indictment. From time to time rumors have placed them in such diverse places as Canada, Cuba, and Algeria. While hiding out, Bernardine Dohrn wrote a "Declaration of a State of War" against what she called "Amerikan imperialism." (Many radicals insist on spelling "America" with a *k*.) The declaration—tape-recorded by Miss

Dohrn and sent to news media in envelopes postmarked in New York—threatened a "symbol or institution of Amerikan injustice" with attack. A short time later the New York City police headquarters sustained a bombing that was generally regarded as the fulfillment of that threat.

An organization calling itself the "Weather Underground" claimed it had committed the bombing that caused the greatest sensation in recent history—the one that damaged seven rooms in the U.S. Capitol Building in the early morning of March 1, 1971. At about 1 A.M. a telephone caller told an operator on the Capitol switchboard that a bomb would soon explode to protest the Nixon administration's war policies. At 1:32 a powerful blast tore through the Senate wing of the Capitol. Explosives experts said the bomb had apparently consisted of fifteen to twenty pounds of dynamite, wired to a delayed-timing device. It had been left in an unmarked, out-of-the-way lavatory about a hundred feet from the Capitol's giant central rotunda. The day after the bombing, various news organizations received copies of a letter from the so-called Weather Underground claiming it had set off the explosion to protest the administration's war policies. The letter had been dated before the bombing, but the copies had been postmarked after it. Thus, investigators were not sure whether the copies had been sent by the actual bombers or by other radicals seeking publicity for an act committed by someone else. There was also uncertainty about whether the Weather Underground—if such an organization existed—was connected with the Weathermen.

Almost two months after the bombing, a nineteen-year-old girl named Leslie Bacon was arrested in Washington and held for questioning in the case. Later she was indicted on a perjury charge for telling a federal grand jury that she had never visited the Capitol Building or grounds. Actually, it was charged, she had visited the Capitol and a House office building the day before the bombing. In August 1972, however, the Justice Department dismissed the indictment rather than reveal in court whether it had used electronic eavesdropping devices in gathering evidence against Miss Bacon. At this writing, the bombing of the Capitol remains unsolved.

Although Miss Bacon denied participating in that bombing, she did concede that she had been a member of a group that had plotted to dynamite or firebomb several buildings in New York. She claimed she "withdrew from all plans more than a month before the actual attempt." Five other members of that group, who were arrested outside a bank identified as one of their targets, pleaded guilty to conspiracy charges and were given prison sentences. In addition to the bank, police said the group had planned to bomb various office buildings, including one that housed a law firm in which President Nixon had formerly been a partner.

Besides bombs that have exploded, many have been discovered and dismantled before doing any damage. Several were mailed to President Nixon, but were found by Secret Service agents and removed from the White House mail room before getting anywhere near the President. Another was discovered in Selective Service headquarters, a block from the White House.

Although most recent bombings seem to have been the work of antiwar groups such as the Weathermen, many others have been attributed to such diverse organizations as the Ku Klux Klan, the Black Panthers, the Jewish Defense League, and a variety of others. Unidentified black militants claimed in an anonymous letter that they had bombed the Louisiana State Capitol in April 1970 in retaliation for the killing of three blacks by the police. In New York thirteen Black Panthers were accused of conspiring to bomb department stores and police stations and to murder policemen. After a trial that lasted eight months, they were found not guilty. One of the defendants, Robert Steele Collier, had previously served a federal prison sentence for conspiring to blow up the Statue of Liberty, the Washington Monument, and the Liberty Bell.

The Black Panthers have been accused of committing numerous murders and assaults on policemen in cities from coast to coast. In turn, they have accused various police departments of trying to kill off their members. In some cases, the Panther charges against the police have appeared to have some basis in fact. In many others the evidence has suggested that there has been a conscious campaign by the Panthers to wage war on the police. Officers have been lured into ambushes, then wantonly murdered. The victims have apparently been chosen at random; black policemen have been shot along with whites.

A Congressional committee conducted an investigation of the Black Panthers and described them as ranting revolutionary radicals "totally incapable" of carrying out their supposed threat to overthrow the government by violence. The Panthers do "pose a serious physical danger to the police and their violent language and conduct create a climate for revolution, even though the Panthers themselves cannot bring about a revolution," the committee said. Congressman Richardson Preyer of North Carolina, who headed the committee, said: "The Panthers wear 'oppression' like a badge. It is their excuse for not making it in society or even trying to make it. It is their too easy excuse for any unlawful or violent act." The late FBI Director J. Edgar Hoover took a much more serious view of the Panthers than the committee. He described the Black Panther Party as the "most dangerous and violence-prone of all extremist groups" in the country.

Many other black militant groups have been accused of

resorting to terrorist tactics. One black leader involved in numerous confrontations over the years, H. Rap Brown, seems to have evolved from an advocate of nonviolent civil disobedience to an exponent of terrorism. Brown got his start in the civil-rights movement as a member and ultimately chairman of the Student Nonviolent Coordinating Committee. After adhering for a time to SNCC's policy of nonviolence, he became an outspoken advocate of "black power"—even if it took violence to achieve it. In one speech, he said violence is "as American as cherry pie." In another, he said, "We must wage guerrilla war on the honkie white man." And in a speech in Cambridge, Maryland, which led to his indictment on charges of inciting blacks to riot and commit arson, he said, "If America doesn't come around, then black people are going to burn it down." Following the speech in Cambridge (which had already been the site of numerous incidents of racial turmoil), blacks went on a rampage that resulted in the burning and destruction of much of the city's black section.

When Brown failed to appear for trial in Maryland after one of his associates was killed in a bomb explosion, he became the object of an international manhunt and was placed on the FBI's list of the ten-most-wanted fugitives. At the time, Brown was appealing a five-year prison sentence in another case, in which he had been convicted of violating the Federal Firearms Act in New Orleans. In addition, he was under indictment on charges of assaulting a federal officer, illegally transporting a gun, and intimidating an FBI agent. On October 16, 1971, after being listed as a fugitive for eighteen months, Brown was wounded in a gun battle with two policemen following an armed robbery at a tavern in New York. He was convicted in 1973 and sentenced to five-to-fifteen years in prison. All told, his record of alleged crimes presents quite a different picture from the one portrayed during his earlier period of nonviolence.

To some observers, H. Rap Brown is far from a respectable or responsible citizen. But many supposedly respectable, responsible citizens have resorted, in the heat of political confrontations, to terrorism that has differed only in degree from Brown's. Consider, for example, members of a group of middle-class homeowners from Forest Hills, New York. When plans were announced for construction of a low-income housing project in their neighborhood—which the homeowners feared would bring in hordes of welfare families—they responded with such acceptable forms of protest as picketing, shouting, and vowing political reprisals against Mayor John Lindsay.

But when they didn't seem to be getting their way, the residents set fire to the temporary headquarters of a construction company that held the contract to build the housing project. In an era of bombings and assassinations, the arson struck some as relatively minor. But the fact that it was committed by presumably decent, law-abiding citizens —whose protest itself was based largely on the fear that lawlessness would invade their neighborhood—gave it a significance beyond the trifling damage sustained. If such "decent" citizens could be persuaded that terrorism is a legitimate means of redressing grievances, one could only wonder what might be the consequences for the future history of confrontation politics.

Similar doubts about the future have been raised by the activities of the Jewish Defense League. Headed by a rabbi named Meir Kahane, the League has presented a startling study in contrasts. On the one hand, its leaders and members have tried to project an image of serious, even scholarly, interest in religious matters. They have taken up, among other things, the cause of Jews who have been denied religious rights in the Soviet Union. And they have conducted lawful demonstrations outside Soviet consulates and offices in various American cities. On the other hand, they have engaged in (or claimed to have engaged in) numerous acts that must be branded as terrorism.

Sniper attacks, bombings, and other such activities have been attributed to members of the League. Rabbi Kahane and seven other League members have been indicted on such charges as assault, rioting, criminal mischief, and burglary. Once, when black militants threatened to disrupt services at a New York synagogue, Rabbi Kahane and a group of his followers stood outside the house of worship armed with clubs and chains to ward off the invaders. The synagogue had not sought and did not want their help. The black militants never showed up. But a picture of the armed League members standing outside the synagogue was distributed throughout the country by the League in an effort to attract recruits. Printed under the picture was the caption "Is this a way for nice Jewish boys to behave?"

Apparently, some Jews thought so. The incident, and distribution of the picture, helped swell the organization's ranks to more than twelve thousand members. With headquarters in New York, it has established branches in Boston, Philadelphia, Cleveland, Los Angeles, and Montreal, and is in the process of creating others.

Many responsible leaders of older Jewish organizations have deplored the activities of the League. Arnold Forster, general counsel of the Anti-Defamation League of B'nai B'rith, a long-time leader in civil-rights and civil-liberties campaigns, has described the strategy employed by Kahane and his followers as counterproductive. "They have served only in confusing the issues and producing results that do not serve the best interests of Jews in Russia or in the United States," Forster said.

A variety of conflicting arguments is available to those who support the resort to violence in confrontation politics and those who oppose it. Supporters argue that revolutionary violence is morally justifiable. They maintain that violence is natural to human behavior—that history has seen a continuing failure to eliminate violence as a means of producing change. They can point to British philosopher John Locke's thesis that when government institutions fail to provide peace, security, and equal opportunity, the right of revolution reverts to the people. They can also point to the words of Thomas Jefferson: "The tree of liberty must be refreshed from time to time with the blood of patriots and tyrants. It is its natural manure." The words of the Declaration of Independence can also be cited: "Whenever any form of government becomes destructive . . . it is the right of the people to alter or abolish it. . . ."

Supporters of violent confrontation argue that violence works. They point out that the United States owes its very existence as a nation to a violent revolution. And most cases in which governments have been successfully overturned, they contend, have involved the use of violence. If government and other powerful institutions will not yield to sweeping change (and the indications are that they rarely will), violence seems to many the most effective way of creating the change.

Those who oppose violent confrontations feel that violence is immoral in a democratic society such as the United States and subverts the nation's ideals. They point out that the essence of a democracy is the citizenry's willingness to accept the decisions of the many, rather than the arrogance of the few. Revolutionary violence, they argue, tears at the fabric of law and order, without which no society can survive. Such violence can lead to anarchy. And, as British philosopher Thomas Hobbes wrote, anarchy is mankind's greatest tyranny because it creates a slavery to fear.

In addition, opponents argue that violent-confrontation tactics do not work in this country. The traditions of respect for law, order, and property are too deeply entrenched in the United States to allow such tactics to succeed. These traditions are bolstered by the fact that most citizens, despite whatever complaints they may have, are basically satisfied with the American system. They have too great a stake in preserving the existing society to permit a violent revolution to succeed. In the absence of large numbers of malcontents, small groups of violent dissidents are easily defeated. Beyond that, opponents of violent confrontation argue that even when violence succeeds, it often produces repression worse than that which came before.

On balance, recent history indicates that violent-confrontation tactics do not work in this country. The bombings committed by antiwar activists, for example, were not responsible for ending the war in Southeast Asia. The bombings and sniper attacks committed by black militants have not improved the lot of blacks in America. The murders and bombings committed by Ku Klux Klansmen and other white segregationists have not slowed the pace of racial integration. The acts of terrorism committed by members of the Jewish Defense League have produced no tangible results.

From all available evidence, the escalation of confrontation politics into terrorism is usually self-defeating. It comes down to violence for the mere sake of violence. And in the politics of confrontation there is no legitimate place for that kind of self-indulgence.

CONCLUSIONS
What Lies Ahead?

DESPITE Irving Howe's description of confrontation politics as "the equivalent in public life of Russian roulette in private life," it does seem to have a legitimate place in American society. There *is* much that is wrong in America today, and the responsible practice of confrontation politics can help bring about meaningful reforms. Certainly, the history of the politics of confrontation has been studded with ample evidence of such reforms.

But what have we learned about the uses of confrontation strategy? What are viable forms of confrontation politics? What tactics are most likely to succeed? And what is the probable future of this sort of political action?

First, as indicated in the previous chapter, it seems clear that resort to violence—whether plotted in advance or spontaneous—is doomed to failure. The days of successful armed revolution in this country are long gone. No band of rebels, no matter how numerous or heavily fortified with weapons, can hope to bring down a government backed by the military might now available to a President. And recent history has shown that even lesser goals than the overthrow of the government have been beyond the reach of those who have resorted to violence to gain political ends.

Fresh evidence of the futility of violence was provided in early 1973 when militant Indians took over by force the village of Wounded Knee, South Dakota, scene of an historic earlier battle between Indians and United States troops. In the 1973 confrontation, the rebellious Indians exchanged thousands of rounds of gunfire not only with FBI agents and federal marshals but also with other Indians who had been driven from their homes and businesses. The ostensible purpose of the violence was to call attention to the needs of Indians and point up the government's many unkept promises to them. It was perhaps partly successful in dramatizing the issues, but the Indians driven from their homes claimed the militants were simply criminals—not true spokesmen for their people. After holding the village for about three months, the militants surrendered without gaining any tangible concessions from the government. The Indians who had been driven out returned to their homes, some of them saying the militants had set back the cause of true justice for Indian people.

What, then, are practical forms of confrontation politics? Some prime examples have been provided by civil-rights and peace activists. Their classic technique has been to confront the establishment with mass protest marches and demonstrations. When the establishment has responded by banning such protests—typically on the ground that required permits have not been obtained—the activists have defied both policemen and court orders and continued their demonstrations. Is this defiance lawlessness? Some critics of confrontation politics insist that it is, but other observers contend it is not if the activities of the protesters are responsible and nonviolent. The denial of permits to protest groups has long been a tactic used by government to squelch dissent. If the only practical way to oppose such a tactic is to violate the orders of policemen and judges—at least for the purpose of forcing a test of the constitutionality of the ban—then it would seem to be a legitimate form of confrontation politics.

But the manner in which the confrontation is carried out usually plays a major role in determining its ultimate legitimacy and success. Refusing to obey police orders by sitting down on a sidewalk, practicing nonviolence and submitting to arrest—favorite tactics of both civil-rights and peace activists—are usually considered legitimate acts of confrontation. They provide demonstrators with clear-cut methods of challenging in the courts the legality of both the original ban on protests and the subsequent arrests. Moreover, if demonstrators make it clear that they are willing to pay the price for their disobedience by going to jail at least temporarily, confrontations can have great moral force. They may help mobilize public opinion behind the causes supported by the protesters. Some critics of confrontation politics have questioned subjecting large numbers of demonstrators to arrest in order to test the constitutionality of protest bans. Wouldn't one arrest, they ask, serve the same purpose in court as many? There is a good deal of validity to the question. But the fact is that mass arrests, in addition to providing the basis for legal challenges, serve to alert the public to the demonstrators' grievances. One arrest, while it may serve the protesters' legal purposes, obviously will not attract the attention of one thousand or five thousand arrests. Dr. Martin Luther King, Jr., was often criticized for his "fill-the-jails" strategy. But there is little question that this strategy—allowing thousands of persons to make their witness by peaceably accepting arrest and imprisonment—was instrumental in the success of the civil-rights movement.

As we have seen, the confrontations that have been most successful have had several ingredients. They have had clearly defined, attainable goals. They have been carried out with careful planning and discipline. And they have been aimed at logical targets—at persons with the power to effect reforms.

Some of the least successful and most disastrous confrontations in recent years have involved protests that ignored one or more of these ingredients. Demonstrations carried out on behalf of outlandish, even outrageous, demands are doomed to end in frustration and possibly in senseless violence. It is the nature of many protesters, particularly young ones, to demand more than they can logically expect to achieve. Within reason, such strategy is acceptable and practical. It gives the other side a chance to save face by granting concessions without appearing to surrender. But when the demands are far beyond reach, they give the other side the opportunity to brand them as frivolous and refuse to budge at all. In addition, those who engage in the politics of confrontation have a responsibility to their followers. If protest leaders make unreasonable demands, without hope of compromise, they may send their supporters into battles that have no ultimate chance of success. Beyond that, they may falsely build up their followers' hopes, which can lead to eventual disillusionment and violence.

Poorly planned, ill-timed, or undisciplined confrontations all carry within them the seeds of disaster. Successful confrontation politics cannot be practiced on an ad-lib, catch-as-catch-can basis. When large groups of people are thrown into the streets without clear purpose or organization, the best that can result is chaos. The worst is catastrophe. Moreover, even if the establishment wants to negotiate, it cannot be expected to do so with a wild mob. Nor can the public at large be expected to sympathize with or support such a mob. Although the words "organization" and "discipline" may seem abhorrent to some militants, they are essential ingredients of successful confrontation politics.

One of the ingredients of practical confrontation strategy most often ignored, at great cost to protest movements, has been the appropriate choice of targets. Students protesting the war in Southeast Asia, for example, often directed their demonstrations at college presidents. Obviously, a college president could not end the war. It is understandable that students want to protest on their own campuses. They cannot rush off to Washington very often to make their views known to the administration and Congress. But by sticking to issues over which the college has control, students can make more effective protests on the campus. For instance, it would be more logical to demand of a college president that he stop allowing campus researchers to work on militarily oriented government projects, or that he halt compulsory ROTC training or campus recruitment for the military services or the Central Intelligence Agency, than it would be to confront him with a general protest to end a war.

Of course, students and other demonstrators may argue justifiably that they should have the right to protest the war or any other grievance when and where they choose. Indeed, they should have that right. The question is how they exercise it. A campus protest against the war is perfectly appropriate so long as it keeps its eye on a reasonable goal. If the goal is merely to make the students' views known to the national administration and the public, that is one thing. But if the goal is to bring about virtually immediate reform, that is quite another. A generalized antiwar protest at Kent State, Berkeley, Columbia, Harvard, the University of Wisconsin, or the University of Texas, or even at all of them simultaneously, cannot reasonably be expected to bring about an immediate cessation of hostilities. For demonstrators to pretend otherwise is to bury their heads in the sand. Over the long run, such demonstrations may prove successful in shifting the nation's foreign policy. But for the short haul, the choice of more localized, appropriate targets promises a greater chance of success.

Where does the politics of confrontation go from here? Recently, various observers, noting a reduction in the number of protests around the country, have predicted that confrontation politics may be on its way to extinction. Those predictions, however, seem grossly premature. Similar forecasts have been made often in the past and have proved inaccurate. After the civil-rights movement's initial wave of fervor, for example, there was a cooling-off period that led some to contend the movement was dead. But when fresh issues arose, new confrontations made it clear that the movement was not merely alive; it was more powerful than ever. Such appears to be the case now with a variety of organizations that have been involved in confrontation politics. They are still alive and looking for the issues around which to stage new confrontations.

Will those confrontations be more or less violent than those in the past? Opinions differ. Some experts believe activists have found violence ineffective and will resort more often to nonviolent tactics. On the other hand, various barometers indicate there may be an increase in violent confrontations. A recent study disclosed that one out of every five American men questioned in a nationwide survey believed some degree of violence was necessary to produce social change in the country. The study was conducted by a team from the University of Michigan's Institute of Social Research. Dr. Monica D. Blumenthal, who helped conduct the study, summarized its findings this way: "The figures indicate that American men think that, where it is necessary, you should reach for a gun fairly fast." Assuming the validity of the study—and there is no reason to question it—the findings show that many Americans still believe strongly in violent confrontation. While no parallel previous study exists to use as a yardstick, the indications are that more Americans believe in such violent confrontations today than did, let us say, ten years ago.

One expert who prepared a policy paper for the National Commission on the Causes and Prevention of Violence, Columbia University Professor Amitai Etzioni, asserted that confrontations have become a permanent feature of the political process and should be regarded as such. "Demonstrations are becoming part of the daily routine of our democracy and its most distinctive mark," Etzioni wrote. "They are a particularly effective mode of political expression, in an age of television, for underprivileged groups and for prodding stalemated bureaucracies into action."

Confrontation, he said, has become an alternative form of political action during long periods between elections, and has permitted protesters to deal with many private power groups not directly responsible to the electorate. "In this sense, demonstrations are becoming for the citizen an avenue like strikes have become for the workers," Etzioni wrote. Carrying the analogy between confrontation politics and employee strikes another step, he predicted that violent confrontations would become less frequent in the same way labor violence did over a period of years. "It should be noted in this context that, as more of the public learned to accept strikes, the occasions on which they erupted into violent confrontations became much less frequent," he said.

Etzioni warned that suppression of all demonstrations "because they are a volatile means of expression would be both impossible under our present form of government and inconsistent with the basic tenets of the democratic system in that it would deprive the citizens of a potential political tool." Contrary to a widely held view that confrontations are a political tool of only a "few dissident factions such as students and Negroes," he wrote, "the number and variety of social groups resorting to this mechanism at least on occasion seems to be increasing." Among those he reported had adopted demonstrations as a means of accomplishing political ends were teachers, doctors, nurses, clergymen, and even some members of law-enforcement agencies.

Ideally, of course, the politics of confrontation would ultimately become so successful that it would phase itself out of existence. If all society's major ills could miraculously be cured, there would seemingly be no further need for confrontation politics—although perhaps human nature is such that there would be malcontents even in Utopia.

The chances of society's ills being eradicated in the foreseeable future, however, seem nonexistent. Thus, a long and possibly tempestuous history lies ahead for the politics of confrontation.

Sources
and Acknowledgments

I HAD the fortune, good or otherwise, to be present during many of the political confrontations described in this book. In some cases, that fortune sent me scurrying out of the way of bullets, buckshot, tear gas, rocks, bottles, and other hazards. First as a newspaperman and during the last eight years as a freelance writer, I have been thrust by my work into the midst of the politics of confrontation. Thus, much of the material in the book comes from personal observation. Other sources have included interviews with numerous public officials, political leaders, law-enforcement officers, judges, lawyers, and, most important, leaders and participants in various protest movements. To all of them, I would like to express my appreciation.

To those in the publishing world who have offered advice, faith, and boundless patience, I am most grateful. The list includes Dorothy Markinko, Ross Claiborne, George Nicholson, Barbara Seuling, Robert Wyatt, Deborah Baker, Ron Buehl, Jane Greenspan, and Cary Ryan.

Once again, thanks are due for moral support from my wife, Jeanne, and daughters, Pamela and Patricia.

In addition to personal observation and interviews, much valuable information was obtained from previously published books. Among those that were most helpful were:

Bishop, Jim, *The Days of Martin Luther King, Jr.* 1971.
Conspiracy, The, by the "Chicago Seven." 1969.
Evans, Rowland, and Robert Novak, *Lyndon B. Johnson: The Exercise of Power*. New York, New American Library, 1968.
Golden, Harry, *Mr. Kennedy and the Negroes*. 1964.
Hartogs, Renatus, and Eric Artzt, *Violence: Causes and Solutions*. 1970.
Johnson, Lyndon B., *The Vantage Point*. 1971.
King, Coretta Scott, *My Life with Martin Luther King, Jr.* New York, Holt, Rinehart & Winston, 1969.
King, Martin Luther, Jr., *Stride Toward Freedom*. New York, Harper & Row, 1958.
Levine, Mark L., George C. McNamee, and Daniel Greenberg, eds., *The Tales of Hoffman*. 1970.
Lomax, Louis E., *The Negro Revolt*. New York, Harper & Row, 1962.
Luce, Phillip A. *The New Left*. 1966.
Mailer, Norman, *The Armies of the Night*. New York, New American Library, 1968.
Michener, James A., *Kent State: What Happened and Why*. 1971.
Miller, Michael V., and Susan Gilmore, eds., *Revolution at Berkeley*. New York, Dial Press, 1965.
National Commission on the Causes and Prevention of Violence, *Rights in Conflict*, a report on the Chicago convention by "the Walker Commission." 1968.
———, *To Establish Justice, To Insure Domestic Tranquility*, the Commission's final report. 1970.
Navasky, Victor, *Kennedy Justice*. New York, Atheneum, 1971.

Powledge, Fred, *Black Power, White Resistance.* 1967.
Report of the National Advisory Commission on Civil Disorders. 1968.
Rubenstein, Richard E., *Rebels in Eden: Mass Political Violence in the United States.* Boston, Little, Brown & Co., 1970.
Schlesinger, Arthur, Jr., *Violence: America in the Sixties.* 1968.
Stone, Chuck, *Black Political Power in America.* Indianapolis, Bobbs-Merrill, 1968.
Warren, Bill, ed., *The Middle of the Country.* 1970.
White, Theodore H., *The Making of the President 1960.* New York, Atheneum, 1961.
———, *The Making of the President 1964.* New York, Atheneum, 1965.
———, *The Making of the President 1968.* New York, Atheneum, 1969.

Index

Abernathy, Ralph, 14, 16–17, 120, 128, 130
Abrams, Creighton, 42, 44
Abzug, Bella, 120
Agnew, Spiro, 130, 140
Anniston, Alabama, 24
Antiwar movement, 117–124
Atlanta, Georgia, 23

Bacon, Leslie, 152–153
Badillo, Herman, 120
Barnett, Ross, 31–36, 40
Beckwith, Byron De La, 53
Berkeley, California, 61–69
Bilorusky, John A., 76
Birmingham, Alabama, 23–24, 25, 47–52
Black, Hugo, 31
Black Panthers, 153–154
Black United Students (BUS), 82, 84–85
Blake, J. F., 8
Blumenthal, Monica D., 166

Bombing, terrorist, 147–154
Boudin, Kathy, 150
Boycotts, 9–18, 50–51
Brown, Edward "Pat," 67
Brown, H. Rap, 155
Brown v. Board of Education, 20, 30
Bujack, Joseph, 85–86

Campus Committee on Political Activity, 65–66
Campus rebellion. *See* Student movement
Canterbury, Robert H., 96, 97
Capitol Building, bombing of, 152–153
Carmichael, Stokely, 117
Carnegie Commission on Higher Education, 76
Carr, Robert, 103
Chamberlain, Wilt, 128, 130
Chicago, Illinois, 131–144
Chicago Peace Council, 132

INDEX

Chicago Seven, 141–142
Civil Rights Act of 1964, 55–56, 57
Civil rights movement, 7–58
Clark, Jim, 56
Clark, Ramsey, 142
Clark, Steve, 129
Cleveland Area Peace Action Committee, 132
Collier, Robert Steele, 154
Colorado State College, 79
Columbia University, 74–75
Communism, 119
Communist Party, 132
Confrontation: definition of, 1–2, 147; nonviolent, 20–21, 29, 57–58, 162–164; targets for, 165–166; violent, 157–159, 161–162, 166–167
Congress of Racial Equality. *See* CORE
Connor, Eugene "Bull," 25, 47–51
CORE, 20–21, 22, 54
Cornell University, 79

Daley, Richard, 138, 139
D'Arazien, Steven, 121
Davis, Rennie, 121, 132, 133–135, 141, 142
DeFluiter, Robert, 85–86
Dellinger, David, 132, 141, 142
Democratic National Convention (1968), 131–144
Demonstrations, 167–168
Desegregation, 7–58
Doar, John, 33
Dohrn, Bernadine Rae, 150, 151–152
Duke University, 102–103
Durham, North Carolina, 21
Dylan, Bob, 148

Ellis, Robert, 33
Etzioni, Amitai, 167
Evers, Charles, 53
Evers, Medgar, 53

Farmer, James, 22, 28
FBI, on Kent State, 104–105
Festival of Life (Chicago), 132–133, 135
Feuer, Lewis, 77–78
Fifth Avenue Peace Parade Committee, 132
Finch College, 103
Flint, Michigan, 151
Font, Louis, 120
"Foolproof Scenario for Student Revolts, A" (Searle), 76–77
Forest Hills, New York, 156
Forster, Arnold, 157
Free Speech Movement, 61–69
Freedom Rides, 22–29. *See also* Sit-ins
Froines, John, 141, 142

Gayle, W. A., 14
Gibbs, Phillip L., 102
Gold, Ted, 150
Goldberg, Arthur (student), 66
Graham, Henry, 44–45
Green, James Earl, 102
Greensboro, North Carolina, 19–21
Guihard, Paul, 37
Gunter, Ray, 38

INDEX

Hayden, Tom, 132, 133, 141, 142
Hobbes, Thomas, 158
Hoefler, Ervin, 88
Hoffman, Abbie, 132, 141, 142
Hoffman, Julius, 142
Hood, Jimmy, 41, 42, 44
Hoover, J. Edgar, 154
Howe, Irving, 2, 113, 161
Humphrey, Hubert, 131, 140

Indians, 162
Institute of Social Research, 166–167
Integration. *See* Desegregation
Interposition, doctrine of, 31–32
Interstate Commerce Commission, 28

Jackson, Mississippi, 28, 52–53, 102
Jackson State College, 102
Jefferson, Thomas, 158
Jewish Defense League, 153, 156–157, 159
Johnson, Jerome, 136
Johnson, Lyndon B., 55–56, 131, 134, 143
Johnson, Paul, 33

Kahane, Meir, 156–157
Katzenbach, Nicholas de B., 35, 38, 42–44
Kennedy, John F., 33–35, 39, 42, 43, 55

Kennedy, Robert F., 26–27, 32–34, 48, 131, 138, 143
Kent, Ohio, 85–89, 105–106
Kent State University, 81–101, 103–113
Kerr, Clark, 65, 67
Kerry, John F., 120
King, A. D., 51–52
King, Coretta Scott, 120
King, Martin Luther, Jr., 10–18, 21, 26–27, 48–52, 55–58, 139, 163
Kirk, Claude, 129
Knowles, Warren P., 71
Krassner, Paul, 132
Krause, Allison, 99–100
Ku Klux Klan, 12, 24, 41, 47, 51, 56, 159
Kunstler, William, 142

Legal Defense Committee, 132
Legislation: anti-riot, 141–143; civil rights, 55–57
Liberty City, 129–130
Lingo, Albert J., 41–42
Liuzzo, Viola, 56
Livingston, David, 120
Locke, John, 158
Lomax, Louis, 19
Lowell, Robert, 118
Lucy, Autherine, 41
Lunine, Myron J., 93

McCarthy, Eugene, 131, 134, 143
Macdonald, Dwight, 118
McGlathery, David, 46

McGovern, George, 143
McShane, James, 26, 33, 34, 36, 38, 42
Mailer, Norman, 117–118
Malone, Vivian J., 41, 42, 44
March on Washington (1963), 54–55
March on Washington (1971), 119–120, 123
Marshall, Burke, 50
Mass arrests, as tactic, 163
Mayday Tribe, 121–123
Meredith, James Howard, 30–40
Meyer, Elmer E., Jr., 79
Meyerson, Martin, 67–68
Miami Beach, Florida, 127–131
Miller, Cecil, 35, 38, 42
Miller, Jeffrey, 99, 100
Mitchell, John, 105, 123
Montgomery, Alabama, 7–18, 25–28
Montgomery Improvement Association, 11, 12, 15

National Association of the Advancement of Colored People (NAACP), 8, 21
National Commission on the Causes and Prevention of Violence, 138, 167
National Lawyers Guild, 132
National Mobilization Committee to End the War in Vietnam, 132, 135
New Left, 72–74. *See also* SDS
New York, New York, 54, 74–75
Nixon, E. D., 9–10

Nixon, Richard M., 123, 130; demonstrators and, 93, 103–104, 106, 111–112, 140; Vietnam War and, 81, 83, 102–103, 143
Nonviolent confrontation, 20–21, 29, 57–58, 162–164
Northwestern University, 79

Oberlin College, 103
Ole Miss. *See* University of Mississippi
Orangeburg, South Carolina, 21–22, 72
Oughton, Diana, 150
Oxford, Mississippi, 30–40

Parks, Rosa, 7–11, 15
Parricide, symbolic, 77–78
Patterson, John, 26, 27
Peace movement. *See* Antiwar movement
Pentagon, march on the, 117–118
Peterson, Richard E., 76
Plant, Chris, 83
Police riots, 136–139
Political confrontations, 127–144
Politics of confrontation, 1–3
Port Huron Statement, 73–74
President's Commission on Campus Unrest, 106–112
Preyer, Richardson, 154
Progressive Labor Party, 132

Republican National Convention (1968), 127–131

INDEX

Rhodes, James, 87, 89, 90–94
Rights in Conflict, 138–139
Rubin, Jerry, 132, 141, 142
Rudd, Mark, 75, 150, 151

Sallot, Jeff, 89
Satrom, LeRoy, 87, 88–89, 90, 94
Savio, Mario, 65–67
Scalapino, Robert, 67
Scheuer, Sandra, 99, 100
Schroeder, William, 99, 100
SCLC, 21, 22
Scranton, William, 106, 110–111
SDS, 73–75, 82–83, 148. *See also* Weathermen
Seale, Bobby, 141
Searle, John R., 76–77
Selma, Alabama, 56
Sharoff, Steve, 84–85
Shelton, Robert, 41
Sit-ins, 19–22, 29. *See also* Freedom Rides
SLID, 73
Smiley, Glenn, 16–17
SNCC, 22, 155
South Carolina State College, 72
Southern Christian Leadership Conference, 21, 22
Spock, Benjamin, 117, 118
Stanford University, 79
Strong, Edward, 63–65, 67
Student League for Industrial Democracy, 73
Student movement, 61–113
Student Nonviolent Coordinating Committee, 22, 155
Students, black, 71–72
Students for a Democratic Society. *See* SDS
"Students for Education," 79
Supreme Court, 16, 20, 28, 30, 31–32

Taft, Robert, 91
Targets for confrontation, 165–166
Terrorism, tactics of, 147–159
Towle, Katherine, 63
Tuscaloosa, Alabama, 40–46

University of Alabama, 40–46
University of Arizona, 103
University of California at Berkeley, 61–69
University of Mississippi, 30–40
University of Nebraska, 103
University of New Mexico, 103
University of Oregon, 79
University of Wisconsin, 71–72, 79, 103

Violent confrontation, 157–159, 161–162, 166–167
Voting, 56–57
Voting Rights Act of 1965, 57

Walker, Daniel, 138
Walker, Edwin, 37, 39
Wallace, George C., 40–46
Washington, D.C., 54–55, 117–124, 152–153

Washoi (confrontation tactic), 135–136
Weather Bureau, 148
Weather Underground, 152
Weathermen, 88, 148–152. *See also* SDS
Weinberg, Jack, 64–65
Weiner, Lee, 141, 142
Weinglass, Leonard, 142
White, Byron, 26
White, Robert, 82, 84–85, 93, 94
White Citizens Council, 12, 14
Whittier College, 102
Widener, Warren, 68–69

Wilkerson, Cathlyn Platt, 150
Willis, Edwin E., 119
Winston-Salem, North Carolina, 21
Wounded Knee, South Dakota, 162

Yippies, 132–133, 135
Young Socialist Party, 132
Youth Against War and Fascism, 132
Youth International Party, 132–133, 135